Social History in Perspective
General Editor: Jeremy Black

Social History in Perspective is a new series of in-depth studies of the many topics in social, cultural and religious history for students. They will give the student clear surveys of the subject and present the most recent research in an accessible way.

PUBLISHED

FORTHCOMING

Titles continued overleaf

Please note that a sister series, *British History in Perspective*, is available
which covers all the key topics in British political history.

SCOTLAND'S SOCIETY AND ECONOMY IN TRANSITION, c.1500–c.1760

IAN D. WHYTE

First published in Great Britain 1997 by
MACMILLAN PRESS LTD
Houndmills, Basingstoke, Hampshire RG21 6XS and London
Companies and representatives throughout the world

A catalogue record for this book is available from the British Library

ISBN 0–333–59760–5 hardback
ISBN 0–333–59761–3 paperback

First published in the United States of America 1997 by
ST MARTIN'S PRESS, INC.,
Scholarly and Reference Division,
175 Fifth Avenue, New York, N.Y. 10010

ISBN 0–312–16514–5

Library of Congress Cataloging-in-Publication Data
Whyte, Ian (Ian D.)
Scotland's society and economy in transition, c1500–c1760/ Ian D.
Whyte
p. cm. — (Social history in perspective)
Includes bibliographical references and index.
ISBN 0–312–16514–5 (cloth : alk. paper)
1. Scotland—Social conditions.   2. Scotland—Economic conditions.
3. Scotland—History. I. Title. II. Series.
HN398.S3W49   1997
306'.09411—dc20   96–29436
                                                        CIP

© Ian D. Whyte 1997

All rights reserved. No reproduction, copy or transmission of this publication may be made without written permission.

No paragraph of this publication may be reproduced, copied or transmitted save with written permission or in accordance with the provisions of the Copyright, Designs and Patents Act 1988, or under the terms of any licence permitting limited copying issued by the Copyright Licensing Agency, 90 Tottenham Court Road, London W1P 9HE.

Any person who does any unauthorised act in relation to this publication may be liable to criminal prosecution and civil claims for damages.

The author has asserted his rights to be identified as the author of this work in accordance with the Copyright, Designs and Patents Act 1988.

This book is printed on paper suitable for recycling and made from fully managed and sustained forest sources.

10   9   8   7   6   5   4   3   2   1
06   05   04   03   02   01   00   99   98   97

Editing and origination by
Aardvark Editorial, Mendham, Suffolk

Printed in Hong Kong

CONTENTS

INTRODUCTION

The last 20 years or so have seen a remarkable surge of new research into the social and economic history of early-modern Scotland, which has led to the questioning of many previous assumptions and a redefining of problems. In the past Scottish history has often been introverted and parochial. 'British' history has frequently been written from an anglocentric viewpoint in which the Scots feature mainly as periodic nuisances: as religious extremists or Jacobite rebels. More recently, however, truly comparative research has explored the similarities and differences between many facets of social, economic, judicial and political structures on either side of the Border, between Scotland and Ireland, and in a wider European context (Devine and Dickson, 1983; Mitchison and Roebuck, 1988; Connolly, Houston and Morris, 1995). The grim view of Scotland in the period between Flodden and the Union of 1707 still lingers on in some popular histories but this major wave of revisionist writing has produced new general histories (Lynch, 1991) and more specialised studies of social and economic history (Whyte, 1995), which have begun to influence the general public as well as the academic world.

This book does not aim to present a comprehensive overview of recent work on social and economic change in Scotland over two and a half centuries. In the space available it would be impossible to cover the full range of important topics adequately. Instead, a number of significant themes has been selected, reflecting distinctive aspects of Scotland's development. Each theme involves a set of relationships: lord and laird, landlord and tenant, kirk and culture, centre and locality, Highland and Lowland, town and country, economic decline and growth, which changed markedly during the period under consideration. Each theme has been a focus for important research in recent years, leading to major re-appraisals. Together they provide a series of interlocking facets illustrating the dynamic nature of Scottish society, its richness and complexity. The differences between Scotland's experience and those of her neighbours, especially England, are brought out here but, equally important, the similarities are also emphasised. However, despite exciting new developments, there is still a vast amount of basic work to be done. Another aim of this book is to highlight some of the key research questions that still require to be tackled.

1

LORD AND LAIRD

Scottish society throughout late-medieval and early-modern times was dominated by landowning magnates, although the form of that domination evolved gradually, as Mitchison (1983) has described it, from lordship to patronage. The Scottish nobility have often been portrayed as barbarous, reactionary and over-powerful in the sixteenth century and as unscrupulous place-seekers in the seventeenth. There has, however, been a major revision of views regarding the relationships between the crown and the magnates in late-medieval Scotland, emphasising co-operation rather than conflict. This, in turn, has changed perceptions on many other aspects of Scotland's society and institutions. One of the most significant themes to run through the period was the tensions that existed within the ranks of the landholders between the nobility and landowners of lesser rank: the lairds or gentry. The supposed steady rise of the lairds to power from the mid-sixteenth century, and the corresponding decline of magnate power and influence, is considered to have caused fundamental changes in the structure of Scottish society and the distribution of power within it. Many aspects of this theory, however, remain untested and the story is a complex one. There has been important new research in recent years into some aspects of the early-modern Scottish nobility, particularly their finances, but both lords and lairds remain remarkably underresearched social groups, particularly in terms of their interactions within the localities.

Scottish Landed Society: Structures and Relationships

In late-medieval Scotland there were around 2,000 heads of noble families, although only about 50, most of them peers, had a significant say in national affairs at any time. Below this were a few hundred substantial landholders who, at their lower end, merged into the peasantry, being differentiated by their tenure rather than by their wealth. The upper level of the nobility, the peers or greater barons, were distinguished by being summoned individually to attend Parliament. The rest of the nobility comprised the baronage, holding directly from the crown but often without titles. Below them were the small barons with lands assessed at 40 shillings of Old Extent or more. The baronetage, an order below the peerage, was created in 1625 to raise revenue for the crown. Baronets were hereditary knights. Lower in status were ordinary knights, a personal rather than hereditary distinction awarded for service to the crown. The nobility comprised a little over 1 per cent of Scotland's population, a figure comparable with contemporary France. On the other hand Scotland had as many peers as England with only about a fifth of the population: 57 in 1603 against 55 for England. An inevitable result was that many Scots nobles were poorer than English gentry. Unlike England, where the peerage was sharply defined and distinguished from the gentry, a Scottish peerage did not emerge until the mid-fifteenth century. Landed society in late-medieval Scotland was more fluid, with greater mobility, than in many other parts of Europe. This blurring of distinctions helps to explain why a Scottish gentry class with a clear sense of identity was so slow to develop.

The Scottish peerage expanded rapidly from the late sixteenth century. In 1603 there were 57 peers. By the death of Charles I there were 119, the largest group of newcomers – 39 – being Lords of Erection who had been granted former church lands. A number of them had been elevated to the peerage for service to the crown. The Scottish peerage expanded more modestly in the later seventeenth and early eighteenth centuries. The Scottish aristocracy was an open élite characterised by both upward and downward mobility. The new peerage of the late sixteenth and early seventeenth century was composed mainly of younger sons of peers and laird families. As in other parts of Europe, including seventeenth-century England, the expansion of the peerage altered the character of the nobility, reducing the degree of wealth and influence considered appropriate for a noblemen.

A notable feature of the Scottish nobility was the persistence of landed families in particular localities over long periods so that families came to be associated with specific regions to a degree that was unusual in England. Grant (1984) has calculated the rates of extinction of Scottish noble families in late-medieval times and compared them with other countries. In England and France the survival rate of noble families was approximately similar. In each 25-year period around a quarter of noble families died out. In Scotland the rate of extinction for dukes and earls was only 16–17 per cent in the second half of the fifteenth century, and for barons and lords of parliament between 5 and 7 per cent. It is possible that the relative lack of internal unrest in late-medieval Scotland compared with England may have encouraged family survival but Grant has suggested that differences in fertility between Scottish and English noble families may also have been important. Marriage with older female heiresses for political and economic advantages may have been less common in Scotland because such heiresses were fewer, so that Scottish magnates were more likely than their English counterparts to marry women of childbearing age, with a greater probability of producing enough sons to carry on the male line.

If the origins of this noble marriage pattern are uncertain, some of its implications are clear. In England the failure of male lines led to a high turnover of landownership. In Scotland the estates of the nobility were more stable and the scope for making large additions to one's territory by marriage much less. In England the acquisition of estates by marriage produced fragmented patterns of landownership, which worked against the strong and continued influence of magnate families in particular localities. The degree of continuity in the occupation of land contributed to stability within Scottish landed society. The fertility of noble families led to a surplus of younger sons who often managed to establish cadet branches. Younger sons were more likely to be granted lands from those already in their fathers' possession than from ones belonging to an heiress mother, a feature which further entrenched families within certain districts.

Greater laird families also established cadet branches, acquisition of feus of church and crown lands, and possibly increasing prosperity with rising prices in the later sixteenth century, allowing them to endow younger sons with land.

The establishment of cadet branches within territories dominated by existing landed families emphasises the importance of kinship in early-modern Scottish landed society. The geographical continuity of landed families helps to explain why kinship remained so important in Scotland long after its role had been reduced elsewhere. Particular surnames came to be identified with specific localities as families' landholdings often remained stable for generations. Scottish society and politics were dominated by the influence of kinship even more than by rank and status. Younger sons of the nobility married into the families of local lairds, which further cemented kinship links within particular localities.

The clearly defined regional spheres of influence of Scottish magnates, which resulted from the geographical concentration of their estates, and the importance of their jurisdictions in baronies and regalities, was powerfully supported by family ties. By the end of the fifteenth century agnatic systems of kinship, recognising relationships only through the male line and defined in their widest terms by the possession of a common surname, were normal. Respect for the surname and family links could give younger sons of lairds a place in the households of powerful noble kinsmen. For most purposes, however, the kin group that was recognised would have been much smaller, possibly extending to third cousins. Kinship recognition also depended on geographical location; remote kin living close at hand might receive as much recognition as close kin living far away. So the Gordons in north east Scotland did not count the Gordons of the Merse as part of their family group. Equally, the Ayrshire branch of the Campbells, while acknowledging the earls of Argyll as their chief, acted largely independently.

Kinship, however, formed only the foundations of magnate power. Their households and retinues formed nuclei of fighting men to provide protection and give status. Even middling lairds might maintain substantial followings in the sixteenth century, like Kennedy of Bargany who kept in his household 24 'gallant gentlemen'. The practice of taking boys from cadet branches into noble households as pages lingered on into the later seventeenth century (Marshall, 1973). Another way in which landed families could strengthen their regional influence was through bonds of manrent, written contracts of allegiance and mutual support between two men, usually a lord and a laird (Wormald, 1985). Such bonds extended the influence of magnates as well as backing up the lairds in their localities by giving them powerful allies. The bonds were not a new development in terms of loyalty so much as the expression of a desire, in an increasingly literacy-conscious age, to confirm existing types of relationship in writing. The relationships involved the extension of values based on kinship to people who were not related. This further emphasises the importance of kinship in early-modern Scottish society and shows how kinship and lordship supported each other. The existence of clearly defined magnate spheres of influence, buttressed by landownership, feudal lordship, kinship and kinship-like ties with non-related families, was one of the most distinctive features of late-medieval Scotland, a system of regionalised power structures that only began to break down in the later sixteenth century. The continuation of an honour society, and the strength of lordship and kinship, helps to explain why lairds were still more dependent on the nobility than their English counterparts.

Below the nobility came the lairds. While there has been little work on the great magnate families of sixteenth- and seventeenth-century Scotland, even less research has been done on landowning families of lesser status. The boundary between the greater lairds and the lesser nobility was less sharp than that between the nobility and gentry of England. In England the gentry were rigidly separated from the nobility and were stratified into knights, esquires and gentlemen, usually with coats of arms to prove their status. In Scotland a coat of arms was not a prerequisite for someone claiming gentry status until the later seventeenth century. Some greater lairds, although lacking a title, had wealth, followings and influence equal to those of many nobles. During the sixteenth century the impoverishment of several noble families and the rise of a number of laird ones further blurred distinctions between the two groups.

Within the laird class there was a wide range of wealth and influence. The feuing of church and crown lands in the sixteenth century increased the uncertainty regarding who was a laird. At the lower end of the scale a laird was normally considered to hold at least two husbandlands (about 52 acres) of land; otherwise he was considered to be a yeoman farmer. No completely satisfactory way of subdividing the lairds has yet been found because of the complex interplay of status, tenure and wealth. Meikle (1988), in her study of the eastern Borders, distinguishes bonnet, lesser and greater lairds. Bonnet lairds, small proprietors, worked their own lands and had little status or influence. Lesser lairds might be freeholders with small baronial jurisdictions but there were also many feuars, vassals of larger landholders, at this level. In the eastern Borders between 1540 and 1603 there were 306 laird families. Fifteen were bonnet lairds, 23 bonnet or lesser lairds, 218 lesser and 40 greater. The lairds in this region married predominantly within their own group and within their own locality. The administration of local government was dominated by laird families. They were challenged at times by powerful non-resident aristocrats but always unsuccessfully.

Most laird families in the eastern Borders remained stable during the second half of the sixteenth century but some, particularly those who had influence and had secured positions at court, prospered and increased their status. Some families were downwardly mobile. Over Scotland as a whole, laird families that held by feu ferme tenure should have increased their wealth during this period as inflation eroded the real value of the feu duties they paid. Although estimating the wealth of members of landed society is difficult, most lairds seem to have prospered modestly with rising prices and additional land. Some were sufficiently well off to build new tower houses or remodel existing ones, in contrast to the gentry on the English side of the Border. By the later sixteenth century both the nobility and the lairds were placing greater value on education. Lairds in the eastern Borders tended to send their sons to schools outside the region, especially in Edinburgh. More lairds' sons from the eastern Borders were sent to university in Scotland and abroad than the sons of gentry from the English side of the Border.

Stresses in Sixteenth-century Landed Society

Sixteenth-century Scotland was characterised by much greater levels of disputes over land than the previous century, in terms of feuds and litigation. While landed society had been fairly stable in the fifteenth century, the sixteenth brought new political, economic and social influences that led to stresses in the relationships between different social groups. This may reflect the strains imposed on feudal structures by influences such as population growth, inflation, the shake-up in the land market, religious upheavals and the rise of the lairds.

In some ways the Reformation strengthened the position of the aristocracy. It removed the clerical state from Parliament and state offices, at least until Charles I's reign. Protestantism also gave the nobles an ideological justification for their position in the state, as godly magistrates, and they benefited more tangibly from the acquisition of church lands. Yet in other respects the Reformation led to a weakening of the hold of the nobility over society. The development of the Calvinist church with its kirk sessions (Chapter 3) gave a greater role locally to lairds and feuars as church elders. The aristocracy could no longer take the leadership of Scottish society for granted as sections of the lairds, lawyers, urban merchant élites and the clergy became more assertive.

This is most evident in terms of political influence. In the later sixteenth century an increasing number of lairds began to make their way independently at court without the aid of noble patrons. Many of the new peerages granted by James VI in recognition of royal service went to men from gentry backgrounds. Did this represent the rise of a new social group to challenge the position of the aristocracy or merely a number of individual opportunists making the most of changed political conditions? In particular, the influence of the greater lairds at court and in royal administration increased in the later sixteenth and early seventeenth centuries while in the localities they began to form the core of a slowly expanding system of local government. James VI promoted many younger sons of lairds at court and many became courtiers in their own right rather than having to depend on aristocratic patrons.

James VI has been credited with a deliberate policy of creating a *noblesse de robe*, a new peerage whose origins lay with lawyers, lairds, and younger sons and cadet branches of the nobility (Lee 1959, 1980). It has been suggested that this nobility of service had a vested interest in the maintenance of royal government that contrasted with the aims of the older nobility. Several historians have emphasised James' preference for men of middling origin, concluding that there was a sharp distinction between the two groups. It does seem as if members of families of the new nobility married within their own circle and only to a limited degree with the old aristocracy, suggesting that they were not yet fully accepted. Nevertheless, in the early seventeenth century the most prominent nobles in politics were the Earl of Dunbar, the younger son of a Border laird, the Earl of Dunfermline, the younger son of a lesser noble, and the Earl of Menteith, also from the lower ranks of the nobility. They were not members of traditional leading magnate families like Douglas, Gordon or Hamilton.

Too much, however, can be made of the distinctiveness of the new nobility; they co-operated rather than clashed with the old nobility and contemporaries did not draw sharp boundaries between the two groups. Nevertheless, the power of the new nobility derived not from lands and followings but from the offices they held. It has been claimed that the gentry were emerging as a more independent and powerful group, although the idea of the 'rise of the lairds' is a theory that requires more rigorous testing. Although over a hundred lairds had attended the Reformation Parliament it was James VI who formally brought them into Parliament in 1587 when two commissioners, with a joint vote, were appointed for most shires. Those eligible to elect the commissioners were freeholders with lands valued at a minimum of 40 shillings of Old Extent, a much higher wealth qualification than the English equivalent. Feuars whose superiors were landowners other rather than the crown did not receive a vote until 1661.

The creation of the shire commissioners in 1587 was an acknowledgement of social changes that had already occurred. The lairds had previously petitioned for separate recognition as an estate in Parliament but they did not achieve this ambition until 1640. The real influence of the lairds lay in their estates and localities. The rise of the shire commissioners in Parliament was nevertheless a slow one. In 1640 their vote was doubled, with one

vote being granted to each of the two commissioners representing most shires, although it was 1681 before all 33 shires were
represented. In 1690 26 new commissioners were distributed
between the shires. Once installed, the shire commissioners soon
began to take an independent line, especially on taxation, using
Parliament to air their grievances to express their resentment at
subsidising the nobility who received pensions from crown
revenues. The shire commissioners and burgh commissioners
formed a coherent block in Parliament, with radical influences
that emerged after 1638, were suppressed but not eliminated
after 1660 and surfaced once more between 1689 and 1707.

A fundamental influence on the position of the nobility in the
late sixteenth and early seventeenth centuries was the growing
power of central government, which began to affect the localities
to a much greater degree than before (Chapter 4). A number of
James VI's policies combined to alter the position of the nobility.
As state bureaucracy increased in size and became more professional, government became a full-time activity, less attractive to
greater magnates who could not afford to abandon their power
bases in their localities. For the early seventeenth century the old
view of a clash between an increasingly beleagured nobility and a
more progressive, absolutist monarchy supported by rising
middling social groups still has adherents. Even so James' success
in increasing his power appears to have been due more to co-
operating with his nobles and winning their support rather than
attacking their power.

The late sixteenth-century nobility continued to enjoy privi-
leged access to the king. People of lesser status could only
approach the monarch through a noble, but the creation of a
new nobility widened the range of those with independent access
to the monarch. There were other potential threats too; Goodare
(1989) has termed the 1590s a period of unprecedented aristocratic paranoia. Proposals for a new royal guard under the
command of a laird might have restricted access to the king;
plans for a reform of the Privy Council might have excluded
nobles. In 1593 a number of nobles reacted to perceived threats
to exclude them from government by staying away, but overall the
nobility saw the advantages of co-operating with the government
rather than opposing it. Nevertheless, as their economic circum-

stances became more difficult in the late sixteenth and early seventeenth centuries, their dependence on the crown increased. Their local client networks, based on land, became less important than securing a place on the bureaucratic gravy train and gaining royal pensions. Their increasingly dependent status must have affected them, and as the seventeenth century progressed it is probable that many nobles felt increasingly alienated and frustrated by the growth of central bureaucracy and their financial dependence on the crown.

Financial Pressures: A Crisis for the Nobility?

There were economic pressures on the nobility too. Brown (1989) has suggested that the confidence of the nobility was shaken by a marked rise in indebtedness during the last two decades of the sixteenth century, coinciding with the period of most rapid price rises, similar in some respects to the crisis that has been claimed for the English nobility. It is possible, of course, that some noble families were in financial difficulties at an earlier date. The later sixteenth century is relatively well documented and this may hide the extent of the impact on magnate finances of the English invasions of the 1540s or the Marian civil wars. Nevertheless, Brown cites examples such as the first Earl of Lothian, who committed suicide because he could not pay his debts, the twelfth Earl of Crawford, who died in a debtor's prison in 1620, and the sixth Lord Sommerville who, having alienated most of his land, gave up using his title because his lifestyle could no longer match the dignity of a peer. These are extreme examples but several other nobles had to sell off part or most of their estates to meet their creditors, while the earls of Argyll and Buccleuch took mercenary service abroad to raise money. A deterioration in the health of the finances of the nobility is likely to have affected perceptions of their status by other social groups. In particular, increasing resort to borrowing money and growing difficulty in repaying it is bound to have altered the image of the nobility among the merchant communities of the larger burghs, which provided so much of the credit.

Why was the late sixteenth century such a bad time for noble finances? The lag between inflation and the rise of money rents outside eastern arable areas (Chapter 2) and the diminution of the real value of feu duty income to lords who had acquired the superiority of church property were two factors. Bad harvests in the 1580s and 90s caused famine conditions that cut the flow of rents to a trickle in some years. Rising standards of living increased noble expenditure and many of the new nobility, with insufficient land and income, may have got into debt through struggling to emulate the lifestyle of the great magnates. This is especially likely after 1603 when landowners may have carried on increasing their expenditure in the expectation that grain prices would continue to rise when, in fact, they levelled off (Macinnes, 1991). Overspending was not confined to the aristocracy; many lairds, especially those with ambitions at court, were also getting seriously into debt in the late sixteenth century.

The growing availability of credit from an increasingly prosperous Edinburgh merchant élite looking for ways of investing their capital may have tempted landowners into overspending. On the other hand it is not clear to what extent landowners were merely taking advantage of a credit boom. There was certainly a major expansion of credit following the Reformation, especially after 1587 when Parliament allowed interest at up to 10 per cent to be charged. Before this usury had, in theory, been illegal, although there were various ways round this. With rising prosperity in the early seventeenth century merchants were keen to lend money as the income from this form of investment could be substantial.

Attendance at court in London after 1603 was ruinously expensive for those nobles who chose to remain courtiers. As feuding gave way to the equally aggressive pastime of pursuing one's neighbour at law, legal expenses, including the cost of staying in Edinburgh while cases were tried, rose rapidly. Rising taxation also began to have an impact towards the end of James VI's reign and to an even greater degree under Charles I. Taxation had been infrequent before 1600. It became more regular after 1607 and virtually annual from 1612. £200,000 Scots was levied between 1600 and 1609 but this rose to £507,000 between 1610 and 1619. The tax of 1621, designed to raise £1.2 million Scots over four years, was greater than the entire tax bill for the previous 50 years. The total taxation imposed between 1620 and

1629, £2.4 million, seemed vast compared with earlier levies but between 1630 and 1639 the figure rose to £4 million.

Whatever the background circumstances, borrowing from other landowners and especially from urban merchants became increasingly common either by bond, involving the payment of an annual rent or interest on the principal sum, or by wadset, in which a loan was secured on land, the lender receiving the use of the land rent-free or at a reduced rate in lieu of interest. Although nobles were able to avoid creditors more easily than people of lesser rank, debts still had to be repaid and ways of increasing noble income were limited. Selling off land to pay one's creditors was a desperate measure but one which was increasingly resorted to. It is not clear whether there was net alienation of lands out of noble hands to landowners lower down the social scale or merely a redistribution within the nobility. Developing the agricultural and industrial resources of estates was another possibility but the ethos of 'improvement' or even merely of more commercial management had yet to pervade the Scottish nobility. There was far less enthusiasm for trade and industry than was shown by major landowners after 1660. Raising rents began to be adopted mainly, it seems, from the 1630s. It has been suggested that, by this time, there was a new, more commercial and aggressive attitude towards estate management but this has yet to be clearly demonstrated (Macinnes, 1991).

Some royal favourites obtained monopolies for particular manufacturing processes but these speculative ventures rarely turned in significant profits. More certain was marriage to an English heiress, a course of action that bolstered the finances of a fortunate few. More generally available, and eagerly sought after, was royal patronage in the form of offices and pensions. Before 1603 the limited finances of the Scottish crown prevented liberal economic patronage but after 1603 James had the far greater revenues of England at his disposal while the Scottish exchequer was relieved of the cost of maintaining a court. By 1617 £120,000 Scots a year was being paid out in pensions and the sum continued to rise after James' death, while new crown offices were an additional source of noble income.

Style and Status

Increasing dependence on the state was accompanied by a decline in the military role of the magnates. With the curbing of feuding and greater controls on the size of retinues and on the use of firearms, the martial image of the nobility began to change. With the reduction and eventual eradication of feuding (Chapter 4) perceptions of lordship altered, with a re-evaluation of the noble code of honour. As was occurring throughout Western Europe, the military rationale of the aristocracy was declining steadily. The lack of a standing army in Scotland and the survival of the medieval concept of the 'common army', raised by sheriffs but in practice a loosely integrated collection of magnate and laird followings, extended their military role into the early seventeenth century (Goodare, 1989). However, the long period of peace before 1638 caused the concept of the common army to wither away.

England had seen a re-evaluation of the noble code of honour more than a generation earlier and the Scottish nobility may have gone through a similar process with the decay of the structures of feudal society. This manifested itself in an increased desire for the same formal regard for status accorded to English noblemen. After 1603 sons of noblemen began using the courtesy title of 'Lord' rather than the traditional designation of 'Master', suggesting increasing concern for deference and respect. Greater contact with the English nobility after 1603 may have helped to generate an identity crisis and inferiority complex among Scottish magnates as they moved from being the leaders of society in an independent nation to a poor, provincial nobility, this generating envy, frustration and ultimately aggression.

The open, informal style of James' court before 1603 had given nobles easy access to the king. After 1603 the nobility lost the ability to apply direct pressure on James. After the first flood southwards of Scots nobles on the make James gave in to English pressure to halt the influx of Scots to the court. Nevertheless, Scottish influence there remained strong. Scots dominated the court for a decade after 1603 and still held a disproportionate number of important court offices under Charles I. Only a minority of Scottish nobles spent long periods at court after 1603 and not all of them became thoroughly anglicised. Scottish courtiers continued to send their sons to university at St Andrews or Glasgow rather than Oxford and Cambridge. They were still concerned about events in Scotland but uninterested in England. Courtiers like the Earl of Panmure invested their gains in Scottish estates and the architecture of their new or refurbished houses remained firmly within the Scottish/continental tradition rather than echoing English architectural styles.

Although only some Scottish nobles who went south after 1603 became thoroughly anglicised, those who spent much of their time at court inevitably came under a new set of influences (Stevenson, 1992). This was emphasised by Patrick Gordon of Ruthven, writing in the late 1640s. Seeking to explain why the Marquis of Montrose had been so successful in mobilising royalist support in Scotland while the Marquis of Huntly had been such a notable failure, he emphasised how Montrose had displayed the traditional values of Scottish aristocratic leadership. Huntly, on the other hand, had spent much of his life at court. His followers were alienated by his English manners, especially what Ruthven described as 'the English devil of keeping state'. Scottish nobles who had been influenced by the English court 'began to keep a distance, as if there were some divinity in them, and gentlemen must therefore put off their shoes, the ground is so holy whereupon they tread'.

Scottish nobles were characteristically informal with their followers and inferiors, just as Scottish monarchs had been with their magnates, in a manner similar to that of France. The Scottish and French courts were designed to allow relatively free access to the monarch. The English court, from the reign of Henry VIII onwards, had been structured to preserve distance between monarchs and their subjects. Scottish informality did not, however, mean lack of recognition of status; 'he is an evil bred gentleman that understands not what distance he should keep with a noble man' wrote Ruthven. Scottish society was strongly hierarchical and status conscious but because in the sixteenth century that hierarchy was universally recognised and was seen to be stable, men of different ranks could treat each other in an informal way. Montrose 'did not seem to affect state, nor to claim reverence nor to keep a distance with gentlemen', while with Huntly 'service done... was forgotten and old servants for whom there was no use must be brushed or rubbed off, as spots from clothes'. This was not Huntly's original character according to Ruthven, but the product of his English upbringing. James VI had deliberately brought Huntly to court to distance him from his power base in north east Scotland. He returned home in 1636 an anglicised stranger, deeply imbued with loyalty to the crown but, ironically, unable to mobilise the Gordons in support of Charles I.

In England codes of manners among the nobility and at court had been growing more formal, stressing the suppression of strong emotions. It has been argued that increasing insecurity about their position made English nobles touchy and more insistent on deference. Such attitudes were spreading downwards through English society from the nobility to the gentry. When James moved south in 1603 English courtiers were appalled at the informal way in which he treated his Scottish cronies. James was quick to adopt a more formal style but he still allowed freer access to his courtiers than Elizabeth had done. By contrast, stiff formality and distancing were carried to an extreme under Charles I, which disturbed and offended even English nobles. The contrast in English and Scottish manners was demonstrated dramatically in 1633 during Charles' disastrous visit to Scotland. The king was deeply offended at the open, friendly, informal approaches of the Scots nobility who were not familiar with court etiquette, while he himself came across as cold, unfriendly and aloof.

The tendency for Scottish nobles to behave with increasing formality in dealing with their inferiors was commented on as early as 1607. The contrast between English and Scottish manners is also clear from comments made by English travellers in early seventeenth-century Scotland. They were surprised, for instance, to see retainers serve their masters and then sit down to eat with them at the same table while still wearing their bonnets. The spread of new modes of behaviour through the upper levels of Scottish society set up stresses. Lords who had absorbed English codes of behaviour were affronted when they did not receive due deference from inferiors, who were in turn shocked that they were not being treated in the traditional manner to which they were accustomed. The slow assimilation of Scottish nobles with the English landed élite became more pronounced in the later seventeenth century but has been little studied.

The Road to Revolution: The Nobility and Charles I

In the early seventeenth century pensions and mercantile credit helped to keep the nobility solvent, especially as inflation slowed down and economic conditions improved. Cuts in patronage under Charles I, along with much higher taxation, deteriorating economic conditions and a drying up of credit, threatened magnate solvency once more. With this background of financial insecurity it is easy to understand the fright that Charles I's proposed revocation scheme caused. In its initial form it seemed to involve all grants of land belonging to the crown or kirk since 1540, whether made during a royal minority or not. This seemed likely to undermine the property rights of virtually every major landowner, threatening in particular those loyal servants of James VI who had been rewarded with church property annexed to the crown. The sweeping scope and vague wording of Charles' revocation, compared with the more limited and precise ones of James V, Mary and James VI, would have meant that, if ratified by Parliament in its original form, no one would have been secure in their property rights. To make things worse previous revocations had been to some degree paper exercises as monarchs did not have the power to implement them fully. The stronger, more distant administration of Charles I was seen as a greater threat.

The balance between lord and laird shifted even further under Charles I who, as well as distancing the nobility from power, attempted in his revocation a form of social engineering that would have freed many lairds from magnate influence. One of his aims was to transfer the feudal superiorities or former church lands from lords of erection to the crown, making the feuars freeholders with eligibility to vote. Charles also promoted the use of the term 'gentry' to refer to untitled barons and freeholders. The revocation also aimed to strengthen another 'middling group', the ministers, by giving them greater stipends. The effects of the price revolution on the real value of feu duties and money rents meant that teinds (tithes) were an increasingly important source of income for larger landowners. Any threat to this, as with the revocation, was bound to provoke magnate reaction. In fact Charles' aims behind the revocation were not as revolutionary as the nobility originally feared but by not seeing fit to explain his purposes he perpetuated anxiety. The revocation was crucial in spreading a climate of dissent, which may have been fuelled by the various background influences mentioned above.

If James had worked with his nobles, despite his reservations about their powers, Charles set out deliberately to undermine the sources of their power. He attempted to break their grip over the Court of Session by banning nobles from sitting on it and, by preventing members of the Court of Session from serving on the Privy Council, make it more docile. He used the Scottish Parliament increasingly to push through unpopular measures by narrow majorities rather than broad consensus. If there is doubt about the extent to which the nobility were alienated by the growing power of James VI there is none about their disillusionment under Charles I. There was an increasing feeling that the aristocracy had no part in Charles' autocratic, distant, alien government and that he was intent on grinding them down.

The Scottish Revolution was led by the nobility, although they had the support of a broad spectrum of society. Their alienation lies at the heart of the problem, but what influences lay at the root of this alienation: economic, social or political? As we have seen, larger landowners may well have experienced economic difficulties early in the seventeenth century with a subsequent improvement in their circumstances. It is not clear how badly they were affected by a renewed economic downturn in the later 1630s (Chapter 7). How much was due to to resentment of their reduced role following the Union? To what degree was resurgent nationalism a spur to protest and revolt? To what extent was their rebellion an attempt to encourage Charles to restore to the nobility the position and patronage which they considered their due, an attempt that unintentionally got out of control? This has been a fruitful area of recent historical debate.

Certainly, the nobility were by now less involved in government than they had been for generations. The key question – why did such a conservative society with a long tradition of social cohesion rebel against its monarch and precipitate civil war in Ireland

and England? – remains hard to answer. We still know too little about the nature of society in early seventeenth-century Scotland to be sure, especially concerning how the structure and the reality of lordship and local government changed. There is some evidence that tensions in Scottish society, from the magnates to the tenants, may have been greater than was once thought. Religion undoubtedly played a part, triggering off the revolution crisis, but it is hard to believe that religious discontent alone motivated the rebellion.

Explanations for the Revolution can be divided into those which take short-, medium- or long-term viewpoints. The short-term theory put forward by Lee (1985) explains the revolution as the direct result of Charles I's political incompetence, with a short, rapid build-up to the crisis beginning as late as 1633. However, Lee overstresses the contrast between James VI's skill as a political manager and his son's manifest inadequacy. He underestimates the degree to which James's judgement and his grasp of conditions in Scotland slipped during his last years, and also the degree to which after 1603 many decisions had come from the Scottish Privy Council rather than from the king. He tends to play down the extent of disillusion among the aristocracy caused by James' absentee rule, as well as the unrest caused by his religious policies, which were designed to make Scotland conform more to English forms of worship. Notwithstanding his undoubted ability, James' personal style of government involved compromises that papered over the cracks in society rather than filling them in, leaving problems for his son.

Medium-term explanations see the roots of revolution going back to the Union of 1603 and attempts, by James as well as Charles, to bring Scottish society and institutions into line with those of England. Changes had been evident under James, even if the English Parliament had sabotaged his efforts to achieve a federal union, but Charles I greatly accelerated the pace of attempts to make Scotland conform to English practices in administrative and economic as well as religious spheres. This caused strains in Scottish society and increased the anglicanisation of religion. The more authoritarian character of government, especially after 1603, clearly altered the relationship between monarch and magnate.

Long-term theories have looked further back for the origins of the Revolution, based on the feeling that the stability of Scottish society cannot have remained unaffected by the religious shifts after the Reformation, political instability, inflation and the shake-up in the land marked caused by feuing, as well as the effects of the Union of 1603. For Makey (1979) the Covenanting movement was an aristocratic reaction against social changes caused as much by inflation as centralizing by the crown. The mid-seventeenth-century revolution was only the final episode in a social revolution that was deeply rooted in Scotland's feudal past, the culmination of a process that had begun over a century earlier. This exacerbated or even outweighed the blunders of Charles I. According to this view Charles' failure was not so much in his policies as in the methods with which he tried to implement them. An 'awe-inspiring degree of crass stupidity' aside, Charles' misfortune may have been to exacerbate latent tensions that already existed in Scottish society rather than creating them from scratch, particularly as regards the alienation of the aristocracy. Weighing up the various viewpoints, it is difficult to accept that relationships between Charles I and the Scottish nobility could have deteriorated so rapidly unless there were already longer-term and deep-seated stresses affecting Scottish society as a whole, and the position of the major landholders in particular.

While Stevenson (1973) has tended to dismiss social factors as influences on the development of the Covenanting movement and Lee (1985) refuses to consider European parallels for the breakdown of government in Scotland, other historians have been concerned to set the Scottish Revolution in a broader context. Cowan (1990) takes to task attempts to exclude Scotland from the wider mid-seventeenth-century European crisis. He considers that there was a general 'crisis' in early seventeenth-century Scotland caused by an absentee king, the Union, changes in the church from 1560, and an aristocracy that saw itself under threat both by changes operating within Scottish society and from attacks by the monarchy. This suggests that Charles I inherited a social structure that was ready to collapse and it has been claimed by Cowan that 'To deny that there was a crisis flies in the face of contemporary opinion'. Makey (1979) suggests that in the early seventeenth century Scottish society was in turmoil and ready to explode. Macinnes (1991) sees the emergence of the Covenanting movement as as much a product of nationalism as of religious and constitutional grievances. The Scottish Revolution was a national revolt similar in character to those in Catalonia and Portugal against Spain. It was, moreover, influenced by theories of Dutch writers and the example of the revolt of Netherlands.

At the outbreak of the Revolution the support of the nobility for Charles I split on lines which, if not entirely court/country, at least reflected an element of this. About a third of the adult Scottish peers in 1638 had held royal appointments or otherwise been closely attached to the court. Almost all of them supported Charles. Many of the Covenanting nobles were younger men who had grown up in a period when the Union was increasingly seen as failing to function. The Revolution was the work of the landed classes and was dominated and led by the aristocracy, although they had the support of all levels of Scottish society. The initial focus of opposition on the new prayer book and religious issues more generally helped the nobility, with their own agenda relating to the restoration of position and patronage, to harness popular support. There was no intention of altering the distribution of power in society. There was, indeed, a radical element in the Covenanting movement but its significance has been exaggerated. The only regime during the Covenanting era not dominated by the nobility was the Kirk Party between September 1648 and September 1650, led by ministers, lawyers and burgesses. This was one of the few periods when the church felt strong enough to pursue the nobility for offences like adultery (Chapter 3).

Even the General Assembly of the Church of Scotland, which met in 1638 to consider religious grievances, was dominated by nobles through the shrewd manipulation of the new office of 'ruling elder'. While the National Covenant was drafted by a lawyer, Archibald Johnston of Wariston, it was written within a framework approved by the nobility. The view of the Covenanting movement as an aristocratic, conservative reaction to Charles I has been challenged by the theory that there was a strong radical element within it right from the start. The centralising policies that were a notable feature of the Covenanting administration (Chapter 4) have been attributed to the political radicalism of the gentry and burgesses as much as to the nobility. In 1648–50 this radical element emerged briefly to dominate the Covenanting movement without the support of the nobility.

The nobility had been driven to oppose crown but in the process they unleashed forces they could not control, which, in the end, destroyed feudal society. By the 1630s magnates who wanted to carry on being kings in their own localities – like the Marquis of Huntly – were being seen as increasingly anachronistic. Although giving members of the nobility command of the regiments raised for the new Covenanting army restored for a time their traditional military role, the Revolution marked the end of the feudal nobility. The defeat of the Engagers led to the discrediting of the nobility who had mostly supported the Engagement. They were no longer trusted, and noble leadership faltered for the first time in the Covenanting wars. The original revolutionary leadership was replaced by more radical leaders from lower levels of society. The nobles began to fear that in destroying the king's party they had destroyed their own and the whole social order.

But even radicals could not contemplate a future without a king and the proclamation of Charles II led to the restoration of the nobility. The failure of the Kirk Party to hold power for long showed that there was no consensus in favour of theocracy and that the country could not be ruled without the nobles and great lairds, malignants or not. There was no adequate alternative base of power. Experience of the Kirk Party drove many nobles and lairds back to support the king to prevent a takeover by extremist ministers. The nobility survived the Kirk Party's regime but then faced an occupying army intent on crushing any royalist opposition.

Restoration and Recovery

The Covenanting wars and Cromwellian occupation wrecked the finances of many landowners through heavy taxes, destruction of property, fines and borrowing. Many nobles had borrowed heavily to contribute to the cause of the Covenant in the late 1630s and the Irish campaigns in the 1640s. Royalists who borrowed money to support their cause were also badly hit and in the 1650s there was massive wadsetting of land to raise cash. The Cromwellian regime set out to destroy the influence of the nobility and give more power to the middling sectors of Scottish society. Nobles were deprived of their offices. Rigorous enforcement of the laws of debt by Cromwellian judges drove many desperate nobles to join Glencairn's rising, provoking further disaster. Although events forced the Cromwellian administration to review this policy, many of Scotland's greatest noble families were bankrupt by the later 1650s. By 1656 Robert Baillie claimed 'Our Nobles lying up in prisons and under forfaultrie or debts... are for the most part either broken or breaking'. Two years later he wrote 'Our Noble families are almost gove; Lennox hes little in Scotland unsold; Hamilton's estate is sold; Argyll can pay little annuel rent for seven or eight hundred thousand merkes... the Gordons are gone, the Douglases little better... many of our chief families... are crashing; nor is there any appearance of any human relief'. In 1661 Charles I's treasurer, the Earl of Traquair, was begging in the streets of Edinburgh.

The Revolution removed the nobility's independent status, leaving them as large landowners who might choose to follow careers in politics. Their exclusion from power in the Cromwellian years, in terms of both central government and their local jurisdictions, had an effect on society that has yet to be fully evaluated. After 1660, for instance, they had much less influence over their tenants in matters like church attendance. Their loss of influence created a vacuum that many lesser landowners filled. During the Covenanting period the lairds had dominated local government through the shire committees of war and the collection of taxes. In the Restoration period the larger lairds were more active in Parliament and played an important part in the assertion of parliamentary independence after 1688.

The Restoration produced a strong royalist reaction. The nobility regained power in central and local government although they no longer seemed so invulnerable and their prestige had been permanently lessened. To control the western Covenanters, legislation in 1678 involved the impounding or arms and horses, even those of magnates like the Duke of Hamilton, who had to petition the king to recover his carriage horses. The nobility had to work hard to rebuild their endebted estates. The Parliament of 1661 lowered interest rates, extended periods for repayment of debts and assigned the lands of some forfeited Covenanting landowners to prominent royalists. Despite these advantages it is still not clear how so many landowners, from magnates like the Duke and Duchess of Hamilton down to the lesser nobility, were able to manage their finances and estates so that by the 1680s many of them were able to embark on ambitious building projects (Marshall, 1973). This apparent economic miracle still requires detailed research. In contrast to the early seventeenth century, when the land market had been very active, less land changed hands in the later seventeenth century, a trend further encouraged by the 1685 entail act. Even so the total number of landowners diminished; there was a decline in the practice of granting property to younger sons, and large estates absorbed the lands of many small proprietors and owner occupiers. The number of landowners in Aberdeenshire fell by 25 per cent in the later seventeenth century and continued to decline during the first three quarters of the eighteenth. The share of the great landowners increased at the expense of small ones rather than the lairds so that by 1771 large landowners owned half the county.

The anglicisation of the Scottish nobility continued through the later seventeenth century, an unobtrusive but significant process that helps to account for their support of the Union of 1707 (Chapter 7). English fashions in clothes and interior furnishings, rather than ones bought in Edinburgh, became essential status symbols, as did English servants in some Scottish noble households (Marshall, 1973). The fashion for new country mansions, which spread through Lowland Scotland in the later seventeenth century, reflected a desire to emulate the English nobility. In the later seventeenth century one Scots peer in seven was marrying an English heiress as a way out of financial difficulties, although the number of marriages was undoubtedly reduced by the reluctance of English noblewomen to live in Scotland. While the fourth Duke of Hamilton was educated at Glasgow University in the later seventeenth- century, the fifth Duke was sent to Eton.

Given their loss of political power and difficult financial circumstances it is not surprising that so many members of the nobility turned to the economic development of their estates. There does not seem to have been a widespread tendency to raise rents but more efficient collecting of existing rents may have helped improve their finances. Agricultural improvement, due to difficult economic conditions and shortage of capital, was possible only on a limited scale. Given the low levels of grain prices it is understandable that many major landowners became involved in the cattle trade, exploiting fisheries, developing new markets and fairs, mining coal and manufacturing salt.

During the later seventeenth century there were growing signs that landowners were developing a more explicit class interest based on the common factor of ownership of property rather than adhering to distinctions based on differences in feudal tenure, which were seen as increasingly irrelevant. Legislation, notably various acts encouraging agricultural improvement, which culminated in the division of commonty and runrig acts of 1695, increasingly emphasised the possession of landed property rather than feudal superiority, stressing the unity and common interests of the landowning class and its division from the tenantry. At a county level growing class solidarity was reflected in an increase in the frequency of meetings of groups of landowners as heritors to take decisions as Justices of the Peace or Commissioners of Supply, including the running of local society. The increasing use of the term 'heritor' to describe any owner of landed property, regardless of tenure, emphasised status based on property rather than feudal superiority.

This process may not have been unconnected with the fact that there were close links between laird families and the legal profession, which had yet to become dominated by entrants from noble families. Lawyers promoted property against the long-standing rights of feudal superiority that were increasingly seen as archaic, but at the same time the rights of property owners were stressed at the expense of lesser people, an example being the law of hypothec, which allowed the removal of tenants' possessions in lieu of rent arrears.

By the early eighteenth century the fortunes of the nobility were firmly linked to English interests. Andrew Fletcher of Saltoun described them as 'greedy, ambitious, and for the most part necessitous men, involved in great debts, burdened with great families, and having titles to support'. The attractions of Union with England were obvious even setting aside the direct and indirect persuasion that was applied to them by the English administration (Chapter 7). Although some nobles had headed south after 1603 and there was an even greater inclination to live in London in the later seventeenth century, when incomes allowed, there was a more significant outflow after the Union of 1707. A high proportion of the first rank nobility based themselves in London, along with many of the greater gentry as MPs in the House of Commons, leaving the lesser nobility and the gentry to run Scotland. After 1707 the attention of the magnates focused more and more on London, leaving local society to be run by the gentry, a pattern that was increasingly like that of England. The eighteenth century in Scottish society can indeed be seen as the century of the lairds, who dominated the law, the economy, culture and society.

The convergence of the Scottish and English landed élites proceeded more rapidly after 1707, with increasing intermarriage as titled Scots sought not only English estates but also, more importantly, English aristocratic influence, which could open up access to top posts in the British civil establishment. By the end of the eighteenth century a truly British ruling class had emerged. However, the focus of the leading nobility on London did not mean that they had relinquished their traditional hold on Scotland, where power still lay in the hands of those who held most land. The difference was that London-based Scottish nobles employed agents in Scotland to conduct their business. The power that such agents had for independent action was strictly limited. This mechanism operated at various levels from the running of individual estates to the wholesale management of Scottish politics by the Earl of Ilay (from 1743 third Duke of Argyll) from 1725 to 1761 (Shaw, 1983). The agents of Scottish magnates were often lawyers and this has led to some mistaken suggestions that the Scottish legal establishment in some way took over the government of Scotland in the first half of the eighteenth century. In fact, as Shaw (1983) has shown, men were appointed as agents on the basis of their social background rather than specifically for their legal expertise. The system of clientship that united lords and lairds in the sixteenth century continued to operate in a very different social setting in the first half of the eighteenth century, with lords dispensing patronage rather than protection.

2

LANDLORD AND TENANT

Throughout early-modern times the pattern of landownership in Lowland Scotland was characterised by the dominance, sometimes over huge areas, of a limited number of large proprietors. Scotland had the most concentrated pattern of landownership in Europe, with important implications for rural society in general. While owner-occupiers and small proprietors were frequent in some areas, notably parts of the western Lowlands, over most of the country there was a huge gulf between those who owned the land and those who worked it. Although there were variations in the land market over time in terms of the amount of property changing hands, when land did become available it tended to do so in large blocks that were acquired by existing landowners. With the exception of areas immediately around the larger towns, little land was offered in small parcels that would have allowed a wealthy tenant to become a small proprietor. The feuing movement of the mid-sixteenth century, discussed below, provided the only mechanism for substantial numbers of tenants to become landowners, and the effects of this were highly localised. Once the feuing movement had ended, opportunities for tenants to become owner-occupiers were negligible. The greatest advancement that the son of a tenant could hope for was, via a university education, to become a minister or a schoolmaster, or to pursue a career in estate management as a factor or chamberlain. Access to the landowning élite was denied to him.

The dominance of the landowning class gave them a degree of power over rural society that was envied elsewhere in Europe. Their feudal jurisdictions of baronies and regalities were maintained into the mid-eighteenth century. Regalities were abolished and the powers of baronies curtailed in 1747 but other feudal survivals, like labour services and thirlage to the estate mill, continued even longer. The predominance of leasehold tenure, increasingly shorn of its customary protection, meant that when conditions were ripe for change in the mid-eighteenth century Scottish landowners were able to transform the countryside and rural society with remarkable speed.

Sixteenth-century Rural Society: The Impact of Feuing and Inflation

Yet in the sixteenth century, while landowners were strongly aware of their position as the heads of local communities and part of more or less extensive kinship and clientage networks, they were not very conscious of being part of a group with common economic and political interests. Scottish society, from noble to cottar, was bound by vertical linkages based on reciprocal obligations of paternalism and deference. There was a good deal of consensus in rural society between landlord and tenant. This was shown in the operation of baron courts and in the birlay courts that sometimes existed under them. Birlaymen, whether elected by the tenantry or appointed by landowners, were reliable men who dealt with disputes between tenants and problems arising from the need of neighbours to co-operate in many aspects of farming. Judgements in sixteenth-century baron courts were commonly given by the suitors as a group or by a jury appointed from among them.

The late survival of feudal structures might suggest that the relationships between landlord and tenant remained little changed before the advent of large-scale improvement from the 1760s transformed the countryside and rural society. Recent research suggests otherwise, although the nature, scale and significance of change in rural society often remain elusive. In the sixteenth century a major agent of change was the feuing of church and crown lands. Feu ferme was a hereditary tenure conferring much greater security of possession than leasehold. A superior who granted land in feu usually required a substantial cash payment and an annual feu duty. This was designed as an economic rent for the land and might be as great as, or greater, than the rent under leasehold. In order to make up for the loss of grassums, lump sums that were often required on the renewal of leases, additional periodic charges might be imposed on the feuar with a double feu duty on the succession of an heir.

Although feuars initially paid heavily for their security, inflation steadily eroded the real value of their feu duties during the second half of the sixteenth century. Because it permanently alienated land from the superior's control, feuing was mainly an emergency expedient for raising money. The main impetus in the 1530s was James V's massive taxation of the church but high taxation continued under the regency of Mary of Guise. The English invasions of the 1540s brought widespread destruction of churches and religious houses in southern and eastern Scotland and more land was feued to rebuild them. Feuing reached a peak in the 1550s and 1560s before tailing off in the following two decades. Overall, it has been suggested, about a third of Scotland was feued out at this period.

The feuing movement has traditionally been seen as a disaster for small men, especially tenants whose customary rights to the continued occupation of their lands were set aside when their land was feued over their heads to rack-renting lairds and nobles. Sanderson's (1982) study of feuing has shown, however, that this is an oversimplification. More than half the feus went to sitting tenants, only about 3 per cent to the nobility and 29 per cent to lairds, many of whom were only small landholders. In terms of the amount of land granted, tenants did less well as many of the feus to lairds and nobles involved big blocks of territory. Nevertheless, large areas of land were transferred out of the hands of the feudal classes to a new social group that lay outside the traditional circle of power. On some estates, like those of Paisley Abbey and Coldingham Priory, over 70 per cent of feus went to the tenants. In parts of northern Ayrshire and Renfrewshire, the Merse, Fife, lowland Perthshire and Banffshire there was a major change in the structure of rural society as many new small proprietors were created.

Becoming a feuar, however modest, encouraged new attitudes towards local society and the world at large. The enhanced status of many feuars was expressed by the construction of new tower houses, clusters of which sprang up in several areas. In some districts the patterns of landownership created during the mid-sixteenth century endured for two centuries or more. The large touns in the Tweed valley, feued to tenants of Coldingham Priory and Melrose Abbey, were still distinctive communities of owner-occupiers, their lands intermingled in a complex pattern of strips and blocks, in the mid-eighteenth century (Dodgshon, 1981). Elsewhere, however, the new pattern of landownership did not remain static for long. Inevitably, some feuars were more successful than others; some sold out while others absorbed the lands of their neighbours. The role of feuing in opening up the land market, and indeed its long-term social impact in different districts, has yet to be explored in detail. Around the larger towns it may have facilitated the purchase of estates by merchants and professional men but it was mainly ambitious local families rather than incomers who engrossed their farms and small estates. The classic example is Alexander Duff of Braco who is said to have stood on a hillside overlooking Strathisla in Banffshire, watching the smoke rising from the tower houses of many small feuars, and to have remarked 'that he would make the smoke of these houses to go through the one vent by and by' (Sanderson, 1982).

Although feuing is the most readily identifiable change in sixteenth-century rural society there were others. Makey (1979) has suggested that there was a silent social revolution in the Scottish countryside resulting from the impact of price inflation, which, combined with changes in land tenure, led to a major redistribution of wealth from the nobility and larger lairds in favour of the smaller lairds, feuars and tenants. While the scale and chronology of sixteenth-century price inflation have now been clearly established by Gibson and Smout (1995) its effects are still not clear. The price of grain and ale rose gently in the first quarter of the sixteenth century, doubled in the second quarter, then rose six times between 1550 and 1600, with much of the rise concentrated in the last two decades of the century. Prices rose much more slowly in the early seventeenth century before levelling off. As feu duties, normally paid in cash, were fixed, their real value diminished steadily during the second half of the sixteenth century, to the benefit of feuars and the detriment of their superiors, first the church and then, after the Reformation, the nobles who were granted ecclesiastical superiorities. This transfer of wealth, Makey suggests, was sufficiently great to undermine the foundations of feudal society.

At the same time, Makey has argued, inflation was having a more widespread effect on the rents of lands held by tenants. In the eastern Lowlands, where there was a strong emphasis on arable farming, rents were paid mainly in kind. They were thus effectively inflation-proof and were only likely to be adjusted if additional land was taken into cultivation or the adoption of new techniques led to a marked improvement in crop yields. In the western Lowlands and the Southern Uplands, with a more pastoral economy, rents in money had long been established. The evidence of the Hamilton estates suggests that, despite depreciation due to inflation, rents were not adjusted upwards in line with prices until the 1630s or later. During the later sixteenth and early seventeenth centuries money rents either remained fixed or were not increased in line with prices. In theory there was nothing to stop a landowner from raising rents at the end of a lease and threatening tenants with eviction if the increase was not paid. In practice force of custom would have worked strongly against such action. There would have been considerable resistance by tenants to raising rents that had been fixed by tradition during periods of relatively stable prices, particularly for land held by customary tenures. Rack-renting was condemned by the church and enduring paternalism would also have made landowners reluctant to raise rents.

Stray pieces of evidence, such as tenants continuing to occupy holdings after their leases had expired or having leases renewed when they were already substantially in arrears, suggests that sixteenth-century estate management was, in commercial terms, often slack. Moreover, landowners may not have realised that a problem existed. Although the scale of price rises was massive in the long term, the upward trend was masked in the short term by sharp fluctuations caused by variations in harvest quality. If the fall in the value of money rents was widespread, the effect should have been a gradual decrease in the real incomes of estate owners and rising prosperity among the tenantry. This has yet to be clearly established, but Makey cites the example of the barony of

Avondale in Lanarkshire where the testaments of tenants, who in the 1630s were still paying the same rents as a century earlier, show that at their death their rent liability was only a tiny fraction of their total wealth.

After this burst of prosperity came the inevitable reaction from landowners. On the Hamilton estates in the 1640s, as leases fell due, Lady Anna, mother of the first duke, tried to force tenants to accept massive rent increases – in some cases a tenfold rise – or to continue at the old rent during their lifetimes only after the payment of a heavy grassum. Makey does not believe that Lady Anna was consciously reacting to the price rise but that she simply needed the money. It is curious though that increases on this scale almost exactly restored rents to their pre-inflation levels. The fact that tenants were able to pay such huge increases may itself indicate that they had previously been very lightly charged and had accumulated substantial amounts of capital. Elsewhere the catching-up process may have been carried out in stages rather than all at once. Even so rent rises on such a huge scale must have seemed oppressive to the tenants and may have generated tensions between them and their landlords. Tension is sometimes seen in the eviction, or attempted eviction, of tenants for refusal to pay new, much higher, rents. Makey has suggested that such stresses lay behind the rise of militant radical Presbyterianism in the western shires, the focus for Covenanting activity after 1660, a movement that was led by small lairds and tenants. There may have been tensions within farming communities as well as between landlord and tenant. A tenant who had been paying rent at a similar level to a neighbour might suddenly have found himself paying ten times as much per unit area as a result of his lease coming up for renewal. Tenants and feuars who had previously enjoyed comparable incomes might have become separated by a much wider gap in wealth.

Rent increases certainly occurred in the early seventeenth century in the eastern Borders. The rental of Ettrick rose from £469 in 1499 to £2763 in 1586 – below the general level of inflation – but rocketed to £22,760 by 1650. This may have reflected not only a catching-up process but also improved marketing opportunities south of the Border after 1603, particularly the sale of mutton and lamb to the coalfield areas of north eastern

England. Subsequent rent rises were modest – to £23,149 by 1696 and £26,964 by 1766. The process affected the Highlands too. On the MacLeod of Dunvegan estates rents rose by 400 per cent in the century from 1498 to 1595, but by 600 per cent between 1595 and 1610, and a further 700 per cent between 1610 and 1640 (Macinnes, 1991). Tenants on Islay complained to the Privy Council in 1613 that heavy new exactions were being imposed.

Makey's theory has been been worked out on the basis of only limited evidence, principally from the Hamilton estates. It is not yet clear how widespread such trends were and he has acknowledged that they are likely to have affected different estates in different regions at different times. Detailed scrutiny of estate papers should reveal evidence of rent increases, the impact of which ought to be detectable in the testaments of tenant farmers. Not all historians are, however, convinced. Macinnes (1991) believes that the nobility were able to make significant commercial adjustments in estate management, increasing their income without major eviction or alienation of their tenants, including the conversion of rents in kind and services to money. Dodgshon (1981) has suggested that cash rents had no customary levels to act as brakes on inflation and that rapidly rising prices and declining income from feuars at this period were likely to have encouraged landowners to squeeze their tenants harder whenever possible.

Prosperity or Poverty?

Set against this picture of a tenantry on the make in the later sixteenth and early seventeenth centuries is evidence that conditions for ordinary farmers became worse. This is most clearly seen with regard to tenure. In the early sixteenth century most farmers seem to have been fairly secure in the occupation of their holdings. Impressions of tenancy conditions at this period have been coloured by John Major's comments in 1519 that short leases, insecurity of tenure and the threat of summary eviction were commonplace. The detailed evidence of estate records, however, suggests otherwise. On the estates of Coupar Angus Abbey in the late fifteenth and early sixteenth centuries a fifth of leases were for life and three quarters for five years or less. By the middle of the century, however, estate policy had changed in favour of longer tenancies. Fifty-eight per cent were for life, and a further 16 per cent for 19 years. Only 26 per cent were for five years or less. On the estates of Arbroath Abbey in the early sixteenth century 55 per cent of tenancies were for life and 37 per cent for 19 years. On the lands of Dunfermline Abbey, Holyrood Abbey and the bishopric of Aberdeen the pattern was similar. Conditions of tenure on lay estates are less clear because documentation is poorer but indications are that they were similar to those on church lands (Sanderson, 1982).

In addition many tenants held their lands not by ordinary leasehold but by forms of customary tenure similar to English copyhold. Rentallers, whose title to a holding was a copy of the entry made in the landlord's rental book, normally held for life. Their land was usually passed on to an heir at the tenant's death or even during his lifetime. Such holdings could also be acquired through marriage. On the estates of Paisley Abbey, in the mid-sixteenth century at least, 64 per cent of the holdings were inherited in this way. Rentallers can be seen as a special category of tenant with greater security but in practice differences between them and ordinary tenants with long leases or 'tacks' were probably minimal. The customary right for heirs of tenants of all categories to succeed was known as 'kindness', tenure based on kinship with the previous owner. It is possible that kindly tenure was a late medieval development relating to conditions when, with a reduced population, labour was at a premium and the bargaining power of tenants relatively great. Kindly tenants might hold their land as rentallers, by leasehold or at will but their right to succeed was widely recognised by local and sometimes central courts. The conclusion is that security of tenure, *de jure* or *de facto*, was widespread in the first half of the sixteenth century. With population growth sluggish and labour possibly in short supply it was in a landowner's interest to keep holdings occupied in this way.

Sanderson (1982) has seen the later sixteenth century as a period of growing insecurity for tenant farmers. Many rentallers had their tenure changed to leasehold and the term itself dropped out of use in the early seventeenth century. The customary principles on which kindly tenure operated also came to be recognised less and less so that this designation also died out. Growing population and increased competition for hold-ings may have shifted the bargaining power in favour of land-lords while the growing centralization and professionalism of the legal system may also have worked against the survival of customary tenures. Many tenants on lands that had been feued over their heads may have had to pay higher rents as the feuars tried to recoup the cost of obtaining their charters.

The amount of eviction and rack-renting that occurred as a result of feuing is not clear. Few cases seem to have reached the courts. Although these could have been the tip of an iceberg, Sanderson has concluded that there was less dislocation than has sometimes been believed. Indeed, Brown (1989) has suggested that the pattern of long leases with fixed rents continued during the late sixteenth century because land-owners, during a period of political instability, were more concerned to maintain men on their estates than to increase rents. He believes that it was the expiry of such leases at varying dates in the early seventeenth century which led to massive increases in rents as a catching-up exercise.

This argues a favourable view of conditions for the tenantry in line with Makey. On the other hand Gibson and Smout (1995) have suggested that landowners introduced systems of short leases in the late sixteenth and early seventeenth centuries in order to respond to rapidly rising prices. Certainly, when estate records become more abundant in the 1620s and 1630s short leases and tenancies at will seem to have been normal. The problem is pinpointing when the change occurred on particular estates, and whether the introduction of short leases was indeed linked to rent increases. It should not be assumed that a change from long to short leases was necessarily a disadvantage to tenants. Firstly, it did not automatically mean insecurity. On the Coupar Abbey estates in the early sixteenth century many short leases were renewals to sitting tenants. Moreover, short leases could provide flexibility, allowing farmers to adjust the sizes of their holdings to their capital resources and the amount of family labour available. Coupar Abbey tenants can be identified moving from one holding to another or adjusting the amount of land they worked without moving, strategies that are similar to those of tenants on the Panmure estates over a century later (Whyte and Whyte, 1984).

It should also be noted that short leases were a feature of estates in the eastern Lowlands where rents, paid predominantly in kind, did not depreciate, as well as in the western Lowlands and upland areas where cash rents were normal. Increases in rent cannot always be taken at face value as evidence of landowners trying to catch up with inflation. The augmentations in many rentals from the late sixteenth and early seventeenth centuries may have related to the intake of more land from waste as a result of population pressure rather than heavier exactions from the existing improved area (Dodgshon, 1981). This was certainly the case with the Lothians during the 1620s when, with rapid growth of population in Edinburgh and an expansion of the city's trade, there was an extension and intensification of cultivation accompanied by substantial rent increases (Whyte, 1979).

It is difficult to believe that the later sixteenth and early seventeenth centuries were a period of prosperity for all tenants. Substantial population growth was occurring and it has been contended that conditions for many tenants, without the security of long leases, possibly with rising rents, and faced with land hunger fuelled by population pressure, may have deteriorated. This seems particularly likely for the last two decades of the sixteenth century when harvest failures, dearth and high grain prices occurred in several years. If the central importance of price inflation in sixteenth-century Scotland has only recently been properly addressed, questions regarding the impact of population pressure on rural society and the agrarian economy have hardly been posed. A growing population should have increased the competition for land, which ought to have driven up rents. Whether larger tenants with greater reserves accumulated as a result of falling real rents were able to benefit from the high prices by involvement in the market is not clear. Sanderson (1982) has detected a tendency towards increasing subdivision of holdings on some church estates in the mid-sixteenth century in contrast with a trend towards holding enlargement earlier in the century. This may reflect the start of population pressure. But whether subdivision of holdings was widespread, creating a tenantry even more on the margins of poverty with a decline in average holding size, has yet to be established.

The increasing financial pressures faced by larger landowners in the late sixteenth and early seventeenth centuries (Chapter 1) may have prompted a change in attitude towards their tenants, with a greater emphasis on meeting rents and, eventually, raising them. A series of parish reports for 1627 included references to farms in the Lothians and the Merse that were rack-rented as high as they could go. Sir Richard Maitland, looking back from the late sixteenth century, saw a changing attitude on the part of landowners towards their tenants (Dodgshon, 1981). Some historians have gained the impression that in the first four decades of the seventeenth century many nobles developed a more hard-nosed commercial attitude towards running their estates. This, however, remains to be clearly substantiated.

While we now have a good idea of general trends in Lowland rural society from the mid-seventeenth century onwards, the later sixteenth and early seventeenth centuries remain something of a mystery and badly need more detailed study. Overall it is likely that at this time some tenants improved their position while conditions for others deteriorated. This is easy to write; what needs to be determined by future research is exactly who benefited or lost out, when, where and why?

Rural Society in the Later Seventeenth Century

The effects on landlord–tenant relationships of the upheavals of the Covenanting wars and Cromwellian occupation also require further study. The thorough militarisation of society, the increase in central control and the marked decline in the power and influence of the greater nobles, not fully restored after 1660, are bound to have had an impact on tenant farmers and their attitudes. The readiness of western Covenanters to defy authority, including their own landlords, suggests a new independence of thought and action.

Later seventeenth-century changes in rural society are better documented and have been more thoroughly studied than those in earlier decades. The more abundant sources for this period provide a clearer picture of the structure of farming communities. The tenantry begin to emerge as a group with marked differences in wealth and status rather than a homogeneous, impoverished mass, although there is ample scope for more detailed research on them. They ranged from smallholders, indistinguishable from cottars save that they held directly from a proprietor, through men working modest holdings mainly with family labour, to prosperous farmers leasing large units and employing several hired servants. There were marked geographical variations in the structure of rural society. In the upland parishes of Aberdeenshire tenants were the most numerous social group, comprising nearly half the poll tax payers in the mid-1690s, while in rural areas of Midlothian they were a small élite accounting for only 12 per cent of taxpayers (Devine, 1994).

The poll tax records bring out some broad regional contrasts in the structure of the tenantry and the sizes of their holdings. In the Lothians and the Merse holdings were relatively large, leased by substantial farmers and worked mainly by hired servants and cottars. A significant minority of tenants in this region were sufficiently wealthy and status-conscious to pay the higher rate of poll tax, which allowed them to be designated as 'gentleman'. In this social and farm structure, although not yet fully commercialised, lay the seeds of the more markedly polarised rural society that emerged during the era of Improvement from the 1760s. The origins of the distinctive farm structures of the Lothians in the 1690s have yet to be determined but the impetus must surely have been the development of the Edinburgh market for agricultural produce, both for direct consumption and for export. The period of rapid growth of Edinburgh's population in the early seventeenth century, accompanied by major expansion of the grain trade and the injection of urban capital into the countryside (Chapter 7), seems a likely time for this system to have emerged but detailed work on estate records to confirm this has yet to be undertaken.

In the late seventeenth century average holding size in Lowland districts became smaller moving from south east Scotland northwards into Angus and Aberdeenshire, and also westwards into Clydesdale and Ayrshire (Dodgshon, 1981; Devine, 1994). The Renfrewshire poll tax returns show a much greater number of small holdings where the tenants were part-time weavers. Within Aberdeenshire average holding size declined, and the proportion of tenants in the tax-paying population rose, from the more fertile arable-oriented areas around Aberdeen into the hills. In general terms holdings tended to be small. The occupiers of many multiple-tenant touns may have held only 30–40 acres of arable land in many parts of the Lowlands. In the North East, where holdings seem to have been smaller, 20–30 acres may have been more normal. Their effective size was further reduced by the subletting of portions of the infield land to cottars. Even in the Lothians there were still many small farms that are likely to have operated on a largely subsistence basis.

In some areas the pattern was different though. In the Southern Uplands, where there was an increasing trend to specialization in sheep farming in the east and cattle rearing in the west, farms were commonly from 500 to 1,000 acres or more in size, although the bulk of this was unimproved rough grazing. The commercial character of sheep farming in this region is shown by the fact that cash rents were being charged as early as the sixteenth century. Before the Union of 1603 the desire of landowners to maintain large followings may have kept holding sizes down. In the course of the seventeenth century there was some reduction in the number of multiple tenancies. However, the need to maintain a subsistence arable element, due to uncertainty about being able to import grain from Lowland areas, reduced the amount of winter fodder available, and hence the size of flocks that farms could carry, while keeping up population due to the employment of cottars and servants for cultivation. The full potential of commercial sheep farming in this area was only realised in the early eighteenth century with the final eradication of multiple tenancy and a massive shift from arable to grass in the valley bottoms as it became easier to bring in grain from the surrounding lowlands. The result of this was the widespread dispossession of cottars and small tenants, many of them moving into the developing Border textile industry (Dodgshon, 1983).

The tenantry was changing during the later seventeenth century, if slowly. In eastern Lowland areas and some parts of the west, rents were still being charged mainly in kind, effectively isolating tenants from all but limited participation in the market. Tenants delivered their grain rents to their landlord's granary or the nearest market centre and its sale was arranged by the proprietor's estate officials. Nevertheless, the commutation of rents in kind to money payments made some progress, particularly around Edinburgh, although the process was piecemeal and partial. Multiple tenancy was also gradually reduced on many Lowland estates in favour of single-tenant farms. Such units were less constrained by the needs of communal working, particularly the intermingling of plots in runrig to ensure a fair distribution of land in terms of both quantity and quality, and were potentially more efficient. Even where multiple tenancy was retained the number of holdings on a farm was often reduced from four or six to two. Multiple tenant farms had probably never been universal. They were, however, getting rarer in the later seventeenth century, accounting for only a quarter to a third of tenancies in many areas. The net effect of this gradual change was to reduce the number of tenants and increase the average size of the holdings that they worked (Whyte, 1979).

Enduring paternalism on the part of landowners and the strength of custom probably ensured that continuity of tenure was normal from lease to lease, generation to generation, on many, if not most, estates. Sometimes this is explicit, as in the instructions regarding the Buccleuch estates' annual land settings at Hawick. Although tenancy at will, renewed annually, was normal, a holding that fell vacant was offered automatically to the tenant's heir. If no son or close relative was willing to take the holding on, it was offered to anyone else on the estate. Only as a last resort was a holding set to an outsider. In such circumstances many tenants must have identified strongly with 'their' land even if, in strict legal terms, they often only held it from year to year.

We know far less about the rural population below the level of the tenantry. Tenants, as rent payers, figure prominently in estate records but the people who worked for them do not. References to them are far fewer and are often complicated by variations in terminology. As Devine (1994) has pointed out, the terms 'subtenant' and 'cottar', although often used interchangeably, are not necessarily synonymous. On the fringes of the Highlands subtenants could be quite substantial farmers, paying a rent to a tenant or middleman who in turn paid a lower rent to the landowner and lived on the difference, something resembling the Highland tacksman system. A similar pattern occurred near Glasgow but here the main tenants were urban merchants, craftsmen and professional men who were speculating modestly in the land market by leasing farms rather than purchasing land.

Cottars held small areas of arable land and some grazing rights from tenant farmers, for which they paid primarily in labour. Their smallholdings might range from half a dozen acres down to a mere garden plot, although the majority seem to have had around one or two acres. Cottars were employed primarily to supply labour at the peak periods of the farming year and were often, in addition, part-time tradesmen. Cottars were less frequent in areas like Renfrewshire where tenanted holdings were small and could be worked mainly with family labour; they were probably most frequent in areas like lowland Aberdeenshire where there were many medium-sized farms.

Cottars had no security of occupation and were often expected to move from farm to farm as dependents of the tenants. They frequently paid dearly, both in labour and in rent, for the small plots that they occupied and although, as has often been emphasised, they had a foothold on the land they had little independence and little chance of upward mobility. Most of the people who undertook day labour in the countryside were cottars. The totally landless, dependent entirely on wage labour, were probably a very small group due to the low wages on offer for day labour and the difficulty of getting enough regular work to support a family by this means alone. A few days' work on the mains or on the policies surrounding the estate mansion would have been a useful bonus to cottar families although in practice they probably often received their payment in kind rather than cash.

Gibson and Smout's (1995) calculation of model household budgets demonstrates the hand-to-mouth nature of existence for cottar families; most of them lived close to the margins of poverty. In order to make ends meet their wives would have had to earn as much as possible from by-employments. Payments for women's work were often pitifully small yet the extra marginal income must often have been decisive in maintaining cottar families, along with the earnings of children from seven or eight years upwards. Children at this age might be hired out as herds and, if their actual earnings were meagre, then at least they did not have to be fed at home.

As well as cottars, male and female farm servants were common. These were usually single men and women, although in the South East married servants, with small plots of land but working full time for a tenant rather than seasonally like a cottar, were found. Unmarried farm servants were hired for six months or a year, living in the tenants' households, and were paid a money wage, as well as receiving their keep. It must have been the normal experience for the children of cottars and many tenants to go into service in their teens. Well fed and with some money to save for the future or remit back to their families, their period of service in adolescence and young adulthood must have seemed like a golden time to many married cottars, struggling to feed their families.

Many small tenants must have been in a similar position, caught in the trap set by too little land. Largely dependent on their own produce for basic subsistence, with only limited involvement in the market, they did not have sufficient land to benefit from years when agricultural prices were higher than average; indeed, they might have had to buy in additional meal to survive, depleting already slender resources. In good years, when prices were low, their limited surpluses would have generated little profit. The chronic under-capitalisation of some tenants is suggested by the survival of a kind of sharecropping tenure, known as 'steelbow' in some areas and 'third and teind' in Roxburghshire, where tenants paid a third of the crop plus a tenth for teinds in return for the landowner providing seed and stock (Dodgshon, 1981).

The evidence of testaments suggests that most farmers operated with slim reserves in the later seventeenth century. On the Panmure estates in Angus 78 per cent of tenants had debts at their death, which, if they had all been called in at once, could only have been met by selling off livestock and equipment. Only a handful had a credit surplus (Whyte and Whyte, 1988). On lowland farms, where rents were paid mainly in grain, the system of reckoning arrears worked against the tenants. Arrears due to a bad harvest were calculated at the high market prices of the year of shortage. These had then to be paid off from the slender profits of succeeding years of sufficiency and low prices. Not all tenants, however, were impoverished. There were opportunities for accumulating capital through moneylending, trading and posts in estate administration.

On the Panmure estates there are indications that during the seventeenth century the ability of smaller tenants to accumulate capital hardly improved but that larger tenants were distinctly better off by the end of the century, probably indicating a widening of divisions within rural society. There was a certain amount of mobility up and down the farming ladder but this was not particularly common. Equally, not many tenants ended up on the poor roll and those who did were mainly smallholders. The various strata within the tenantry seem to have been fairly entrenched and it does not seem to have been easy for a man to work his way up from modest beginnings to occupy one of the larger farms. This in turn emphasises the importance of inherited wealth, whether as cash or farming stock. The sums of money owing in testaments indicates that there was flourishing trade within rural society and an active money economy. Some tenants, even cottars, died in posession of substantial sums of ready cash or money out on loan. Cottars lent to tenants, tenants to lairds and even nobles. Larger tenants also drew on urban capital (Whyte and Whyte, 1984, 1988).

Towards 'Improvement'

While the tenants of larger holdings may have been growing more prosperous in the early eighteenth century, conditions for cottars and small farmers did not improve until much later. There was a gradual rise in grain prices from about 1705, and in cattle prices from the 1740s, but any gains for small tenants would have been marginal (Gibson and Smout, 1995). More important, by the mid-eighteenth century, was the increased opportunity for women to earn some money in spinning linen yarn or other forms of rural textile manufacture, such as stocking knitting in the North East.

During the seventeenth, and more particularly the first half of the eighteenth century, the relationship between landowners and rural communities altered. This was partly a result of landowners developing a clearer class interest (Chapter 1). As they came to see themselves as members of a ruling class, not just as leaders of local society or part of a network of kinship and patronage, their relationships with the people on their estates became based increasingly on command and less on consensus. This is reflected during the seventeenth century in the increasingly authoritarian character of baron courts. Judgements by the suitors or a jury gave way to decisions imposed by the baron or his baillie. In the early eighteenth century the baron court, as an institution, withered, being identified with tradition and seen increasingly as a barrier to progress. The spread of an 'improving' ideology among the Scottish landed classes in the first half of the eighteenth century involved the rejection of traditional ways based on consensus within the community and an increasing willingness to initiate restructuring of rural society as well as farming systems. While tenants may have become more prosperous during this period, the revolution in manners and material conditions among the landowners that began to be evident in the 1720s may have widened the gulf between the two groups.

The first half of the eightenth century, as Devine (1994) has shown, saw a slow acceleration of the trends in leasing policy, rents and farm structure that had already been evident in the later seventeenth century. Long leases for 19 years became increasingly common; indeed, they were standard on some estates. Of more significance for the development of the agrarian economy and rural society was the conversion of rents in kind to money on a more widespread basis, integrating increasing numbers of farmers more fully with the market. Commutation seems to have started to gather momentum in the 1730s and spread widely in the 1740s and 50s. This must have slowly led to a more commercially oriented tenantry but the reasons behind the change are not clear. Devine has suggested that the stagnation of grain prices may have encouraged landowners to transfer the responsibility and problems of marketing on to their tenants. This may well have been so but it begs the question, why did landowners not try this in the later seventeenth century when prices were even more static? At the same time numbers of multiple tenancies were steadily reduced on many estates so that single-tenant farms had become the norm by the 1760s, allowing more efficient management of the land. This trend, allied to the conversion of rents in kind, must have encouraged greater market orientation by increasing average holding size. It was also important in facilitating the large-scale enclosure of land that began in the 1760s.

The changes outlined above are likely to have had a considerable aggregate effect on the nature and orientation of rural society. Yet because they were introduced gradually there was no major social disruption. Displacement of tenants was slow and piecemeal rather than the large-scale dispossession that some writers have claimed took place. On a group of estates in mixed farming and dairying areas studied by Devine the average reduction in the total number of tenancies, for periods varying from the mid-eighteenth to the mid-nineteenth century, was around 16 per cent and the worst about 26 per cent. Reductions on this scale, spread over several decades, would have created relatively little social stress. There was much more continuity in tenant structure from the early eighteenth century into the period of improvement than has been realised. It was only in upland areas that major displacement of tenants occurred, in areas like the Borders, Upper Clydesdale and south Ayrshire, as arable farming in such marginal areas became increasingly uneconomic and market pressures pushed estate owners towards commercial livestock production. Here was the Lowland equivalent of the Highland Clearances. The displacement of tenants in Galloway did, however, lead to a full-scale agrarian revolt in 1724–25. The slightly panicky reaction to the Levellers' Revolt shown by landowners in other parts of Scotland, including improvers like Sir Archibald Grant of Monymusk, suggests that tensions between landlord and tenant did exist. This is also implied by references in estate records for Monymusk and elsewhere to damage suffered by landowners through activities like pilfering, arson, damage to planting and property and trespassing, indicative perhaps of covert protest (Whatley, 1990).

The cottar system began to come under widespread attack as the move towards larger farms encouraged a more rational and efficient use of labour. With the development of more intensive farming systems labour was needed on a regular basis throughout the year rather than at a few peak periods, and the economics of granting two or three acres of land to cottar families was increasingly questioned. Removing cottars, absorbing their holdings into the farm, and relying instead on paid farm servants, made economic sense as long as it was possible to hire extra labour at harvest time. This was increasingly available from the new estate villages and older kirktouns as well as from small towns and manufacturing centres. Migrant labour from the Highlands was also used. On the estate of Buchanan in Stirlingshire the system of recruiting large numbers of cottars on an occasional basis to undertake day labouring had given way by the middle of the century to one in which smaller numbers of labourers were employed for most of the year (Gibson, 1990).

As with the reduction of tenants the removal of the cottars was accomplished without major social unrest. Yet, over a period of two generations, rural society became much more markedly polarised as well as more commercially oriented. Some tenants, or more probably their sons, would have found that they could no longer obtain a holding and would have had to settle for cottar status or find alternative occupations. Tenants who kept their holdings and even took on additional land started to accumulate capital on a scale that contrasted with the more hand-to-mouth conditions of the late seventeenth century. The rise of a relatively prosperous proto-capitalist farming class, ready to work with landowners on improvement for their mutual benefit, was already well advanced by the 1750s. By continuing and intensifying the trends that were already evident in the later seventeenth century, landowners in the first six decades of the eighteenth century instituted many of the changes that made possible rapid improvement with dramatic social and landscape change in the last four decades.

* * *

It is clear that it was the much-criticised tenants themselves who carried out a lot of the process of improvement. By the 1740s a group of 'bourgeois' farmers, increasingly literate and well educated, and with some capital behind them, was beginning to emerge. In the 1760s and 70s an increasing number of enter-prising men within this group were willing to take the initiative regarding improvement when encouraged by their landlords, and even to invest their own capital as well as labour provided that adequate security was given. Much of the transformation of Scottish rural society that occurred in the decades after the 1760s was generated from within the farming community rather than being imposed from above.

3

KIRK AND CULTURE

Religion, since the Reformation of 1560, has been seen by historians as a distinctive and fundamental aspect of Scottish identity and Scottish culture. Following loss of independence in 1707 religion has been a key element in preserving Scottish national consciousness (Brown, 1987). The Reformation was certainly an event of major political importance, arguably the most significant watershed in early-modern Scottish history. It also had economic dimensions. The Calvinist emphasis of Scottish Protestantism has been viewed as a force that encouraged Scotland's dramatic economic growth in the eighteenth century. Marshall (1981) has attempted to show that Calvinist doctrines encouraged entrepreneurship in seventeenth-century Scotland. Calvinism has been used to explain supposedly Scottish personality traits like dourness, thrift and a desire to succeed. Nevertheless, it is the impact of the Reformed church on Scottish society that has been seen as most fundamental and lasting. The power of puritanical Presbyterianism has been portrayed as a negative and ruthlessly repressive force, which impoverished popular culture and turned seventeenth-century Scotland into a cultural wilderness. Yet there is an apparent paradox here as at the same time the kirk has been credited with introducing a system of education which, even if its virtues have been exaggerated, produced a society in which, by the later seventeenth century, levels of literacy were relatively high by European standards.

The Impact of the Reformation on Society

The new church appealed particularly to middling groups in society: lairds, feuars, larger tenants and burgesses. It was from their ranks that many of the new ministers were drawn. The ministers came to form a new social élite that identified with the middle ranks of society rather than with its traditional feudal leaders. By the middle of the seventeenth century ministers had started to become a self-perpetuating caste, with son following father into the church. They were also an increasingly wealthy group. In the years immediately after the Reformation stipends were generally modest but they were increased steadily in value, particularly in the first half of the seventeenth century when inflation was low. Ordinary stipends rose from £333 in 1617 to £533 in 1627, with some ministers receiving much more. Edinburgh's ministers were paid £1,200 a year and even some rural ministers got over £900 (Makey, 1979). This, along with income from glebe lands, often made them the wealthiest men in their parishes after the major landowner, on a par with, or better off than, many lairds.

The Reformed church brought a far closer interest in the lives of ordinary people than its predecessor. This attention was focused on the parish community and, as we will see in Chapter 4, the parish began to replace the barony as a community focus. In the later sixteenth and seventeenth centuries most Lowland rural parishes, although often larger in area than their English counterparts, had populations of only around 500–700, a size of community that was easily supervised by a church that, as ties of kinship and lordship weakened, took over many of their functions. In the earliest days of the Reformation the involvement of local communities in the affairs of their churches was at its greatest. Congregations gathered around the table with their ministers at Communion. They elected their own elders and could censure, even depose, their ministers. Gradually, this egalitarian system altered as elders were appointed for life, not annually, and often became self-perpetuating cliques, while many functions such as maintaining the fabric of the church, manse and school, and paying the minister's stipend and the schoolmaster's salary, became the responsibility of the heritors of the parish rather than the entire congregation.

The early Reformed church was not especially puritan in character. It was only with the spread of Andrew Melville's ideas after 1574 that there was a more sustained attack on many aspects of popular culture, including the celebration of religious festivals and stricter Sabbatarianism. It is in this area, along with the kirk's strict control of parish society, that its discipline seems harshest as middle-class values were forced on the lower orders of society in a way which often seems smug and narrow minded. In the Calvinist view salvation could only manifest itself in a society that was consciously godly in its principles. It thus became the business of the church to regulate the lives of everyone, sometimes to an obsessive and unhealthy degree.

The most important instruments of community control developed by the new church were its kirk sessions. These aimed to regulate morals and manners of the inhabitants to promote a godly society. They were a strong agent of social control and regulation. They developed what has sometimes been seen as a moral and spiritual tyranny over everyday life. Mitchison and Leneman (1989) believe that virtually every unmarried pregnancy that reached a fairly advanced state would have been investigated by them. By about 1620 most parishes, except those in more remote parts of the Highlands, had active kirk sessions enforcing strict moral discipline.

Kirk sessions comprised the minister and the elected elders of a parish sitting, often weekly, as a tribunal, before which people were called and interrogated. The elders were chosen from the most prominent men in the community, often smaller landowners and more prosperous tenants in rural parishes, and craftsmen, merchants and lawyers in the burghs. Kirk sessions' procedures resembled those of the High Court of Justiciary and because of this their evidence was acceptable to the central criminal court. People were presumed guilty until proven innocent. Remorseless interrogation of witnesses and defendants proceeded until a session was sure that the truth had been reached. They might deny a midwife to a woman in labour until she named the father, or the child might be refused baptism.

A sizable proportion of the population of a community might expect to appear before the session at some point. In St Andrews between 1560 and 1600 about 1,000 cases of sexual misconduct were dealt with in a town whose population can only have been around 4,000. Elders usually had defined areas of their parish to keep under observation, acting as a kind of moral police force. Their powers within their community were sweeping. Accompanied by a witness, elders could enter people's houses if they suspected that an offence was being committed or a fugitive from discipline harboured. People could be accused of crimes in the street. In Aberdeen on the spot fines were imposed for offences like swearing (Smith, 1985). There was considerable co-operation between individual kirk sessions, which meant that fugitives from church discipline were often tracked down and punished. Ministers used presbytery meetings to obtain information about people who had fled to neighbouring parishes. It was not unknown for kirk sessions to advertise in newspapers for information about absconders. The system of issuing certificates of good moral conduct, given to people leaving a parish and required before settlement elsewhere was allowed, represented a further element of control, as did the sessions' management of poor relief.

The most frequent types of case that they dealt with were sexual, especially fornication and adultery. Sabbath breaking, drunkenness, swearing and slander accounted for most of the rest. The St Andrews kirk session in the later sixteenth century dealt with around 60 cases a year. Fifty-seven per cent involved sexual offences and 29 per cent disorderly conduct. Of the sexual misdemeanors fornication formed the bulk, followed by adultery, with a handful of cases of incest. Penalties imposed by kirk sessions usually involved fines that generally went into the parish poor box, a case of the randy supporting the needy. They also included a ritual of public humiliation designed to shame culprits into better behaviour. This usually consisted of sitting on the stool of repentance in church on Sundays, the number of appearances being proportional to the seriousness of the offence. More serious cases might involve the culprit being forced to wear sackcloth or being placed in the jougs, an iron neck collar fastened to the outside wall of the church or churchyard, prior to sitting on the stool.

Punishments for fornication usually involved a fine and three appearances on the stool of repentance – six times for a relapse. Adulterers might be on the stool weekly for up to nine months. People who showed no contrition or who could not pay a fine might be imprisoned in the church steeple for up to two weeks and those considered beyond redemption banished from the community. Slander cases also appeared on the stool. Sabbath breaking included selling and drinking ale, working and travelling. With the rise of the kirk sessions the practice of handfasting, or sleeping together after betrothal, died out. Something as minor as a young man and woman being seen together in the wrong place at the wrong time could result in a charge of 'scandalous carriage', a term which seems to have included much of what would have been accepted in England as normal courtship. On the other hand church discipline was not meant to be simply punitive; ministers and sessions took great trouble to ascertain that offenders understood properly the nature of their sin and were truly repentant.

The success of the kirk sessions was partly due to their co-operation with the secular courts. There was sometimes an overlap in the kinds of cases tried by kirk sessions and baron courts but the same people were often involved in running each court, with elders also acting as the baillies and officers of baron courts. There was no clear-cut division between crimes and sins. Indeed, following the Reformation, as in other parts of Europe, a range of sins became crimes: adultery in 1563, fornication in 1567, Sabbath breaking in 1579 and drunkenness in 1617. People excommunicated by the church continued to receive additional civil penalties until 1690.

The degree of social control exerted by kirk sessions probably reached a peak between the 1620s and the later seventeenth century. The disruptions of the 1640s and 1650s may have prevented some kirk sessions from maintaining their hold over their parishioners. Some of their authority was lost after the Restoration when sessions were instructed not to meet until they had been authorised by the newly appointed bishops, producing in some cases a gap of two or three years in their operation. A decline in the number of cases dealt with by many kirk sessions from this time suggests that they may have lost some of their efficiency. The opposition of Covenanters also created problems during the Restoration era. The late seventeenth-century register for the parish of Tweedsmuir contains the entry 'No session kept by reason of all the elders being at conventicles'. After the Revolution of 1688, with the re-establishment of a Presbyterian system, there was a further hiatus in the operation of many sessions. From the second quarter of the eighteenth century schism in the kirk increased with the growth of dissenting congregations at a time when some of the functions of kirk sessions were being taken over by Justices of the Peace. In 1712 Parliament withdrew from kirk sessions the power to discipline people of other faiths when Episcopalians were granted freedom of worship.

Few people questioned the right of kirk sessions to punish them, especially as they were supported by the secular authorities. The power of kirk sessions is shown by the fact that most men admitted paternity even though there was no means of proof if they denied it. If a stubborn (or innocent) man refused to admit guilt he would be brought before the presbytery and required to swear his innocence under oath. If he did this he was deemed innocent and discharged, but this procedure usually broke all but the most recalcitrant of fathers.

Poor relief also came within the remit of kirk sessions, on an official basis from 1592, largely by default as they were the only organisations capable of administering it. Funds for poor relief came mainly from voluntary collections each Sunday, from fines levied on those who offended against kirk discipline and from occasional bequests. Landowners strongly resisted any attempts to impose regular 'stents' or assessments on them based on their income from rents. Relief was provided to resident poor, sometimes on a regular basis, more often occasionally. The amount available was insufficient to provide recipients with even a bare subsistence: it was designed as a supplement to earnings and charity from family, friends and neighbours. Payments were also made to non-resident poor. Although the basic mechanism of providing poor relief was fairly standard there were wide variations even between adjacent parishes in the way in which such funds were managed. Some parishes kept a substantial proportion of their poor fund ready to hand and disbursed it relatively liberally. Others loaned out much of their money in order to maximise income from interest and were unable, or unwilling, to respond to sudden increases in demand following bad harvests.

Kirk sessions continued to exert a strong, although lessening, influence over communities throughout the first three quarters of the eighteenth century, with a sharp decline in their power from the 1780s. It is easy, however, to present the apparatus of Scottish kirk sessions as more monolithic and formidable than was perhaps the case. There were no kirk sessions at all for most of the Highlands. Even in the Lowlands, despite the remarkable uniformity of policies that they adopted, there must have been variations in the efficiency of sessions in different parishes at different times depending upon the zeal of individual ministers and groups of elders. In the Episcopalian North East, after the Revolution of 1688–90, higher levels of illegitimacy than in other regions suggests that people were less intimidated by church discipline than elsewhere. In the South West, with its strong individualist Covenanter tradition, the percentage of men admitting paternity in cases of fornication was far lower than elsewhere in the Lowlands. Detailed studies of kirk session records in particular districts may reveal contrasts in the ways in which individual sessions operated.

Some social groups, notably major landowners, their servants and the vagrant poor, were able, on account of their wealth and power on one hand and their mobility on the other, to avoid church discipline. Even within the middle range of society a substantial minority defied the kirk. It has often been assumed that the repressive influence of the kirk led to an impoverishment of popular culture, especially during the seventeenth century. However, we still know very little about this topic, one which is wide open to enquiry by researchers prepared to pose the right questions and sift through local records in search of answers. We need to know more about not just what people did but also what activities like recreation, leisure and festivities meant to them. In the Highlands, beyond reach of the kirk sessions, a semi-pagan form of religion survived into the eighteenth century with a wealth of ancient beliefs and superstitions and a rich oral and musical culture. Even in the Lowlands elements of paganism survived the Reformation.

The kirk may have been less successful than has sometimes been supposed in stamping out traces of the old religion and the elements of paganism that it had incorporated. It should be remembered that Protestantism originally took root most readily in the towns and that the Reformed kirk was not a significant presence in some rural areas before the early seventeenth century. Saints' days, supposedly abolished at the Reformation, continued to be celebrated, while New Year replaced Christmas as an excuse for heavy drinking. In the Highlands preparing the seed, harvesting and grinding the grain all involved rituals of sun movement to ensure abundance. Similar rituals were connected with livestock farming: driving stock sunwise around a fire to cure or protect them. In the Lowlands fire rituals are well recorded in the sixteenth and seventeenth centuries.

Parliament tried, in 1581, to stop fire rituals, well dressing, guizers and other traditional customs. Fire rituals were especially associated with Beltane (1st May), midsummer, and St Michael's Eve (the end of September); bonfires were lit on local hilltops, ritual circuits were made of land or house in a sunwise direction and the fire was lit in the hearth for the next year. Despite attempted bans by central and local institutions these rituals continued into the eighteenth century and remained sufficiently established in popular custom: the baron court of Pitcaple in Aberdeenshire in 1686 imposed a fine of £20 on outgoing tenants who let their fires go out (Dodgshon, 1988). The kirk session of the East Lothian parish of Yester in 1671 recorded that parishioners had been consulting a wizard in the Canongate to help them recover stolen property. Belief in charming and white magic was evidently still widespread.

In the burghs the Reformation brought to an end civic ceremonies like Corpus Christi processions, a change that must have been all the more marked because many such ceremonies were relatively recent institutions, but elements of civic ceremony continued to define the urban social hierarchy (Lynch, 1987). Despite the iron hand of the kirk there seems to have been an underground culture of bawdy literature and song extending back into the seventeenth century and forward to the songs of Burns' 'Merry Muses'.

It is difficult to determine just how much religion meant to ordinary people and how strong their faith was. We have very little information so far on church attendance in early-modern Scotland. Attendance at church and obedience to the moral code imposed by kirk sessions may, of course, indicate conformity rather than genuine belief. Brown (1987) has claimed that in the seventeenth and early eighteenth centuries only about a fifth of the adult population in many parishes actually took communion and that church attendance on other occasions may have been equally poor. This suggests that, contrary to popular belief, church attendance cannot have been universal. Perhaps because people were compelled to conform due to the all-pervasive influence of the church at parish level regular attendance by other than a hard core of devotees was not considered necessary. The size of many parish churches in both rural and urban areas in relation to parish populations and the extent of many parishes, with a considerable distance between the kirk and outlying touns, also suggests this, although the system of elders scattered through the various settlements in a parish meant that all people were in touch with kirk discipline. Despite the limited space in many kirks and the steady growth of population it was not until the end of the eighteenth century that serious pressure on accommodation appears to have been felt. On the other hand Houston (1994) has suggested that much higher percentages of people took communion than Brown has estimated, although his argument is based on evidence from a single parish, Canongate in Edinburgh. He considers that attending church and taking communion was viewed as the basic minimum required to achieve acceptability and respectability in a community. Parents were certainly keen to baptise their children quickly and church attendance is likely to have had important social and cultural as well as religious dimensions.

Education and the Church

The development of an improved education system has been seen as one of the major positive contributions of the Reformed church to Scottish culture. Lack of source material may have led to an underestimation of the number of schools that existed in pre-Reformation Scotland but the reformers saw a clear need for a greatly improved and standardised education system so that people could read scripture for themselves. Such a desire was common among contemporary religious reformers but in Scotland the church was able to enlist the support of the state for its educational programme in contrast to England where, until the nineteenth century, the system depended on charity and private fees. Despite this, progress was slow. In its first decades the Reformed church inevitably gave priority to setting up the new parish ministry, with education taking second place. In 1616 the Privy Council supported the Reformers' aims by requiring that every parish should have a school and a suitably qualified master financed by the local inhabitants. The act was ratified in 1633, and in 1646 it was stipulated that the costs of providing education in each parish should be met by the heritors. This act was axed after the Restoration, however, and its provisions were not restored until 1696.

The 1696 act was the real watershed as it not only legislated for a system of parish schools funded by landowners (who were allowed to recoup half the costs from their tenants) but also included measures for enforcement. Inevitably, provision lagged badly behind the legislation but numbers of functioning schools in the Lowlands nevertheless seem to have increased substantially during the seventeenth century. By the 1690s many Lowland parishes had schools with schoolmasters funded partly by the heritors and partly by fees. There were also unofficial schools, funded solely by fees, whose number has probably been underestimated.

Nevertheless, the suggestion that most Lowland parishes had schools by the end of the seventeenth century is over-optimistic. In areas like the Lothians and Fife this was true but in Galloway, for example, there were virtually no schools outside the burghs at the end of the seventeenth century and half the rural parishes still lacked them in the 1740s and later. To enumerate schools and schoolmasters is one thing, to evaluate their impact is another. What did the schools attempt to teach, how effective were they, and what proportion of the population did they reach? Schoolmasters were not generously paid and their salaries, contributed by the heritors, were often in arrears. It is not surprising that schoolmasters were difficult to recruit or that their educational standards were often low. Reliance on legislative optimism rather than reality has led some historians to paint too bright a picture of the achievements of Scottish education in the seventeenth and early eighteenth centuries, especially compared with England. In practice the differences between the two systems, and the results that they produced in terms of basic literacy, were less than has often been suggested.

The efforts of church and state to promote education should not be seen as altruistic. Education was another means by which people could be controlled and encouraged to conform by being indoctrinated into suitably passive attitudes. The curriculum, which for most people involved learning their catechism and reading from the Bible, prepared children for a life of obedience to church discipline.

In the mid-nineteenth century Scotland had higher levels of literacy than other parts of Britain and the Scottish education system was seen as a model to be emulated south of the Border. From this it was believed that the Scottish system had also been superior in the seventeenth and eighteenth centuries. Scottish education at this period has been seen as cheap and widely accessible to the lower orders of society, promoting equality of opportunity and encouraging the selection of gifted individuals for upward social mobility. This, it has often been claimed, produced one of the most literate societies in Europe, one in which virtually every adult in the Lowlands could write by the mid-seventeenth century.

Research by Houston (1985) on literacy levels in Scotland has revised this picture, showing that while the Scots did enjoy fairly high levels of literacy in the seventeenth century they were not exceptional by European standards. Literacy in Lowland Scotland was no better than in Northern England, with about 75 per cent male illiteracy around 1640 and 35 per cent by 1760. Nevertheless, for a small, poor country this was a considerable achievement. Not surprisingly, levels of literacy varied considerably between social groups, between men and women, town and countryside, and from one region to another. Literacy levels seem to have been fairly stable between the Reformation and the mid-seventeenth century, suggesting that the short-term impact of the Reformation on education was limited. A marked improvement seems to have occurred in the later seventeenth century, particularly among middling social groups like craftsmen and tenant farmers, sharpening the contrast between their literacy levels and those of cottars and labourers, which stagnated. The bulk of the improvement which was discernible by the mid-nineteenth century must have come late. By European standards Scotland had a relatively literate population in the early eighteenth century, on a par with England, Holland and Sweden, at a time when the importance of literacy was increasing. By this time some burgh schools were responding to changing needs by starting to teach subjects like navigation, bookkeeping and geography as well as the traditional curriculum.

By the end of the seventeenth century Scottish universities were also responding to the needs of a changing society. After the Reformation the main task of the Scottish universities was to produce the graduates required for the ministry and for the legal profession in an increasingly litigious society. Although a new college was established in Edinburgh in 1582 to add to those at Aberdeen, St Andrews and Glasgow, few alterations were made to their traditional medieval arts curricula during the sixteenth and early seventeenth centuries. Although the early eighteenth century has usually been identified as a period of significant change at Edinburgh and Glasgow universities, Emerson (1995) has shown that there were important developments during the Restoration period. Until the 1660s the teaching of natural science was still largely based on Aristotle but between then and the end of the century there were rapid developments with the ideas of Brahe, Kepler and Newton, among others, becoming accepted and taught. Further signs of change began to appear in the late seventeenth century with advances in the teaching of medicine, notably at Edinburgh, and in mathematics, science and law, reflecting external demands generated by Scottish society. The most notable and far-reaching reform was instituted at Edinburgh in 1708 when William Carstares abolished the restrictive system of regenting and replaced it by a professorial structure allowing greater specialisation by staff and the teaching of a wider range of subjects. Glasgow followed Edinburgh in 1727, St Andrews and Aberdeen more belatedly. This gave Edinburgh and Glasgow universities a lead that helped to make them the key centres of the Scottish Enlightenment. Academic specialisation was also encouraged by the foundation of many new chairs at Glasgow and especially at Edinburgh. Scottish universities were highly cost effective compared with Oxford and Cambridge and students were more varied socially, with a substiantial proportion from the middle ranks of society and occasional poor scholars.

The Kirk under Pressure

The Union of 1707 guaranteed the maintenance of the established Presbyterian Church of Scotland. With loss of political independence the kirk became a focus for national consciousness, although it is exaggerating to claim, as some have done, that the General Assembly became a surrogate for Parliament after 1707. Although Calvinist doctrines were still strong in the Church of Scotland, the first half of the eighteenth century saw the gradual spread of more liberal influences, with an increasing emphasis on spirituality, charity and tolerance rather than dogma. There was a lessening of religious tension after the upheavals surrounding the religious settlement of 1690. The restoration of Presbyterianism included a change in the system of patronage, the right to nominate ministers to particular parishes. Instead of being in the hands of an individual, usually a noble, patronage was granted to the elders and Protestant heritors of a parish, subject to the approval of the congregation. The most striking aspect of this was that it gave Episcopalian landowners a say in the appointment of Presbyterian ministers, demonstrating that, in terms of Whig ideology, land was seen as more important than doctrine.

The Revolution settlement could not, however, embrace all the shades of belief that existed within the kirk. Two pieces of legislation passed in 1712 were particularly controversial. One granted religious tolerance to Episcopalians, who were allowed to hold their own services and use their own service book. The other, disregarding the Treaty of Union, restored the rights of patrons to appoint ministers to parishes. Patronage led to increasing numbers of disputes, particularly from the 1730s, when patrons tried to install ministers against the wishes of the bulk of the congregation.

Landowners were also diverging from the rest of parish congregations in other ways which became a focus for popular resentment. They began to alter traditional liturgical practices, failed to provide enough pews or new churches, and started to shift an increasing financial burden of church upkeep on to ordinary people. The crown was patron of about a quarter of the parishes in Scotland and political managers were usually careful not to install ministers who would be unpopular with the local community. Most disputes arose between stubborn aristocrats and equally awkward congregations or kirk sessions. Although social differentiation had always been evident among parishioners, it had been minimised by the practice of congregations sitting through the service on stools which they brought themselves rather than in fixed pews. During the early eighteenth century social distinctions became more apparent as landowners began to distance themselves from the rest of the congregation by constructing 'laird's lofts' for themselves and their families. Proprietors increasingly claimed the right to annex a proportion of floorspace in their local churches equivalent to the amount of the land that they held in the parish. They then erected their own pews and allocated the seats in them. The sudden changes in seating arrangements that accompanied the introduction of pews often created major stresses in parish society. Agricultural and industrial changes were already threatening the cohesiveness of communities and causing increasing social differentiation. The allocation of pews to tenants meant that relatively few seats were left for people like rural tradesmen who were not 'attached' to any particular landowner. Competition for non-allocated rented pews pushed rents up and began to deny many poorer people the opportunity to worship in their own parish church, inevitably alienating them (Brown, 1987).

Until this time dissent had been a force operating within the Church of Scotland. In the later sixteenth and seventeenth centuries there was no nonconformism of the type that existed in England. The only people not adhering to the kirk were limited numbers of Catholics in the North East and the West Highlands. Dissident groups like the Covenanters in the later seventeenth century had not sought to leave the kirk but to contest its leadership, their concern being with what they saw as laxity in the church and the nature of its relationship with the state. The patronage issue, which gave rise to virtual pitched battles between congregations and the authorities in some parishes, caused the first proper split in 1733 when the Secession Church, with its focus in Perthshire, Fife and Stirlingshire, broke away. At first only four ministers were involved but its popularity grew rapidly, with many people leaving the established church in the 1760s and 70s.

The Secession Church spread out from central Scotland into rural parishes throughout the Lowlands south of the Tay, absorbing the bulk of the people in the South West who still adhered to the old Covenanting tradition. Estimates of up to 100,000 members by the late 1760s may be exaggerated but support was nevertheless considerable. The four congregations of 1733 grew to 45 by 1750 and over 200 by 1785. Popular religious enthusiasm was also evident in a series of revival meetings, the first one held at Cambuslang in 1742, emphasising free grace (Smout, 1982). The Secession Church, even more than the Evangelicals within the kirk, continued the traditions of the Covenanting movement, with strong moral discipline, fiery preaching and days of fasting. Seceders have been seen as reactionary, ill educated, uncultured, uncouth and anti-establishment, continuing to practise a stern form of kirk discipline after it had lapsed elsewhere. There was a strong connexion between secession and economic change, linked to the spread of agricultural improvement. Dissenters were often upwardly mobile skilled farm workers and tradesmen.

Was more general social protest channelled into church protests and dissent? Brown (1993) believes that the church provided a vehicle for expressing many of the antagonisms that existed within a society which was starting to change rapidly. He sees patronage disputes as the Scottish equivalent of rural protest in the rest of Britain, linked to social tensions generated by agricultural improvement. In a sense this was a continuation of an earlier tradition. During the Restoration period the struggles of the Covenanters combined social with religious protest. It is possible to see the Covenanters' ideology, based on religious persecution, moving in the second quarter of the eighteenth century to a more broadly based concern with social change. Social and economic change caused schism, as did resentment of landowners' authoritarian control of the church. Despite this the kirk still dominated Scotland in terms of nominal adherence. From about 95 per cent at the start of the eighteenth century it had only slipped to about 89 per cent by the late 1760s. Even so the process had been started which would weaken the authority of the kirk and reduce the strength of religion as a force in Scottish society.

At the same time a struggle for control of the Church of Scotland was starting to develop. During the 1740s a group of young ministers was increasingly troubled by the rising tide of disputes within the church and the ease with which the authority of the General Assembly was being flouted. They were solidly Whig and pro-Hanoverian; several of them had seen active service on the government side during the 1745 rebellion. In 1751 they came together at a meeting that led to the formation of the Moderate Party within the kirk. The Moderates, although never in a majority, succeeded in dominating the kirk from the 1750s until 1833, partly through skilful use of the gentry vote. They emphasised the need for order and subordination to authority within the church. Whether justifiable or not, patronage should be accepted as it was the law, in order to prevent confrontation with the government. This was the price that had to be paid for an independent church continuing to occupy a central place in Scottish life. The Moderates wanted the kirk to be free of government control but to achieve this it had to show the political establishment that it could act responsibly (Sher, 1986).

At a broader level the Moderates rejected the severity and narrowness of traditional Calvinism. They did not consider that sermons on predestination helped people to lead more Christian lives. They condemned the harsh Calvinist tradition of strict church discipline and fiery preaching but were accused by their opponents of 'lukewarmness' in religion, being more interested in philosophy than religion, and too concerned to cultivate the airs and manners of gentlemen. Realising that there was little future for a church that remained negative, backward-looking and rigidly dogmatic, the Moderates encouraged involvement in literature and philosophy in an attempt to integrate the church with a society that was becoming more secular and more concerned with matters like economic development rather than theological issues. They aimed to replace the stereotype of the Scottish Presbyterian minister as intolerant, fanatical and ignorant with an image that emphasised style, refinement and good taste. The Moderates aligned themselves with the British ruling élite and were influenced by English views of religious toleration, adopting English models of taste, culture and elegance.

Due to their close association with the landowning élite and the government leading Moderate ministers were appointed to positions of influence that allowed them to manipulate the General Assembly. The success of the Moderates made the kirk, and Scottish society as a whole, more liberal and more open to new cultural and intellectual trends. Moderate ministers like William Robertson and Adam Ferguson played a key role in the

Englightenment. A more humanitarian attitude towards sexual offences is evident in the church by the mid-eighteenth century, coupled with a concern that fear of kirk session discipline might encourage crimes like infanticide. Belief in the value of public penance gradually declined in the mid- and later eighteenth century. Buying oneself out of penance became increasingly common from the 1750s, while more and more men refused to admit paternity in cases of fornication and prosecutions for Sabbath breaking declined. The opponents of the Moderates within the kirk, the Popular Party or Evangelicals, had an appeal that was comparable in many ways to that of the Methodists in contemporary England. They attracted much grass roots support from ordinary people who were being threatened by economic change.

Towards Enlightenment

From the 1740s a group of Scots based mainly in Edinburgh and Glasgow gained increasing recognition in an intellectual movement, of major importance in European terms and unmatched in England, which has become known as the Scottish Enlightenment. It might seem surprising that such an intellectual revolution could have occurred in a small, poor country where Calvinism remained strong. In particular, such a flowering might seem improbable given that the previous century has often been presented as a cultural dark age under the iron discipline of the kirk, preoccupied with arid theological controversy and torn by political faction. This would seem to be confirmed by the execution of a student, Thomas Aikenhead, for blasphemy as late as 1697. However, Aikenhead had been publicly outspoken and abusive in his views over a long period. Other students who expressed similar opinions in a less strident manner were let off.

The view of seventeenth-century Scotland as a cultural wilderness has been shown by more recent research to be a caricature that ignores important intellectual achievements in both the early and later seventeenth century, and also the gradual reorientation of Calvinism, paving the way for a more liberal and tolerant society. The origins of the Enlightenment can now be set securely in the seventeenth century rather than the eighteenth. Partly because of Scotland's smallness and poverty Scots were in frequent contact with the Continent. The number of Scots graduating annually at Leiden more than trebled between the 1660s and the 1720s. Many Scots were educated abroad after attending Scottish universities. Wealthier landowners sent their sons on foreign tours, while merchants brought back new ideas and books. Opponents of James VII and, later, many Jacobites spent periods of enforced exile abroad. Intellectual stimuli reached Scotland from many sources including the Netherlands, France, Scandinavia and, of course, England.

In the sixteenth century royal courts had provided patronage for both the arts and sciences. For a time in the later seventeenth century the residence of James, Duke of York, in Edinburgh created a mini-court that generated patronage and helped to encourage cultural developments in the city (Ouston, 1985). Some of the leading figures in this movement were aristocratic dilettantes. More significantly, however, intellectual developments were also linked to a group of Edinburgh professional men, lawyers and doctors, reflecting the rising status and growing aspirations of the city's middle classes. Achievements were particularly significant in law and medicine, but were also important in the sciences.

The idea that there was a 'royalist enlightenment' in Scotland in the 1680s is an exaggeration but the degree of cultural change among the upper levels of Scottish society in the Restoration era has only recently begun to be appreciated. Emerson's (1995) survey of the libraries of prominent Scottish lawyers, doctors and even ministers demonstrates a broadening of their range of intellectual interests during this period, something also highlighted by the upsurge in publishing that occurred, especially after 1688 when the average number of titles printed in Scotland each year doubled, with a notable increase in titles relating to science.

Few of these works filtered down to ordinary people. However, popular literature was far from being exclusively devotional. Chapbooks produced in England were in widespread circulation. An almanac printed in Aberdeen from the 1680s sold over 50,000 copies a year. In this period the outlook of Scottish intellectuals was converging increasingly with that of English contemporaries, a process hard to identify but which may have been an important precondition for the Scots to make the Union of 1707 work to their advantage (Chapter 7).

Despite the disruption caused by the Revolution of 1688–90 the impetus of the Restoration period carried over into the early eighteenth century. The shift in the domination of Scottish culture from the nobility towards the professions became more marked, particularly after 1707 when aristocratic aspirations became more firmly fixed on London. The Enlightenment was essentially a middle-class phenomenon drawn from closely-knit professional and laird families.

The Scottish Enlightenment remains an enigma in many ways. It is possible to indicate the broader frameworks of social and economic change in mid-eighteenth-century Scotland that provided the setting for the Englightenment but much more elusive are its actual causes. There has been little agreement regarding its definition or timespan. Narrow definitions restrict it to advances in moral philosophy, historical sociology and political economy exemplified by the works of half a dozen writers. Wider definitions encompass achievements in the fields of medicine, science, art, literature and architecture. Too broad a definition blunts the impact of the Enlightenment but narrow definitions fail to set it in context. A consideration of the social and cultural *milieu* in which men like David Hume and Adam Smith lived is essential for a proper understanding of their achievement. The occurrence of so many men of ability within such a small country and brief timespan could be dismissed as a random fluke. But genius is hardly likely to flourish unless important preconditions exist to encourage it. Hume would not have had the freedom in, say, the 1690s, to express the ideas he did half a century later. The changes in the attitude of the kirk in the first half of the eighteenth century were important first, in not stifling the talent of such men and, eventually, in positively encouraging it.

One influence on Scottish intellectual life was the increasing spread of English influences through Scottish society after 1707. There was a desire to emulate and imitate their more prosperous southern neighbours but at the same time to equal and if possible surpass them. A sense of inferiority is reflected in the efforts of men like David Hume and William Robertson to purge their prose style and speech of Scotticisms as they realised that they would not otherwise be taken seriously south of the Border.

The key intellectual developments that led to the Enlightenment were centred in Edinburgh and to a lesser extent Glasgow. The study of the origins of the Englightenment is thus in great measure the study of the development of culture and society in these two cities from the later seventeenth century. In the late seventeenth century Edinburgh developed as a social centre for the gentry and nobility as well as an important centre for educating their children (Chapter 6). Foreign wars and losses incurred in the Darien venture may have encouraged more Scottish landowners to stay at home rather than go abroad. This favoured the development of a winter social season in Edinburgh with concerts, dances and other activities. A new charter in 1688 envisaged a large-scale programme of civic improvement with government aid for new public buildings and streets. Although these ideas only came to fruition in the second half of the eighteenth century, it is significant that they were circulating at this time.

Edinburgh continued to develop as a social centre in the early eighteenth century. The Assembly Rooms opened for dances in 1710. The Musical Society, founded in 1728, held weekly concerts for much of the year. Scotland's first newspapers, the Edinburgh Evening Courant and the Caledonian Mercury, appeared in 1718 and 1720 respectively. Allan Ramsay's circulating library, dating from 1725, was the first in Scotland. Edinburgh was fast becoming an important centre of book publishing in European, not merely British, terms. Plans to improve the city, which developed into the creation of the New Town, went alongside sustained civic interest in the promotion of the university, still seen as the 'toun's college', as another way of enhancing Edinburgh's prestige.

Despite these institutional developments much of the socialising that was an integral part of the Enlightenment took place in Edinburgh taverns. The major figures of the Enlightenment all knew each other, many since childhood or student days. Edinburgh provided a *milieu* that was large enough to offer a range of professional positions in law, the church, medicine and education and plenty of social attractions but at the same time still small, tight-knit and familiar, unlike contemporary London or Paris.

* * *

By the mid-eighteenth century Scottish society had moved a long way from its seventeenth-century image of oppression by a dour and dominant kirk. Hard line Calvinism still had a wide popular following but during the first half of the century, under the influence of internal trends and influences from south of the Border, the traditional stern discipline had started to relax. By the 1760s the Moderate leaders of the church were aligning it in a new direction that not only permitted but also positively encouraged wider intellectual horizons. In doing so the church provided a setting that made the Enlightenment possible and, indeed, contributed positively to it. In the process, however, the church opened itself up to challenges that led to religious pluralism in Scotland for the first time since the Reformation and which, ultimately, greatly weakened its influence over society.

4

CENTRE AND LOCALITY

Sixteenth-century Scottish society was fragmented and decentralised into a multiplicity of localities on which central authority impinged only lightly. Change to a more centralised state with increasing interference and direction from the government and professional judiciary only began to gather momentum towards the end of the sixteenth century. Nevertheless, despite increasing central control, Scottish society and many of its key institutions remained decentralised to a degree which surprised English observers and which has often been interpreted as backward, inefficient and weak.

Localities, Communities and Franchises

The nature of Scottish communities remains elusive, although, remarkably, there have been few detailed studies of particular localities and the nature of social interactions within them. This remains one of the most fertile fields for future research in Scottish social history. It is, however, evident that in the sixteenth and seventeenth centuries there were no 'county communities' comparable with those of England. There was not enough of an administrative or judicial focus at sheriffdom level to generate them until the early eighteenth century and then only in a weak form. What did exist were 'family communities' in which particular localities were dominated by one or more landed families tied together by kinship and feudal relationships. Such communities were dynamic and complex, rarely static.

Below the level of the landowning families the farming population identified with their locality and its dominant families
through reciprocal ties of paternalism and deference, distant
kinship and the operation of local courts. Individual family
communities might be united under the regional influence of
magnates like the Gordon earls of Huntly. Meikle's (1988) study
of the eastern Borders between 1540 and 1603 has shown that the
spheres of influence of family communities were quite distinct. A
family that acquired land within an area dominated by another
might have been able to collect rent from it but to move there
and try to build up a power base was a dangerous course of action
likely to lead to confrontation. Laird family communities in this
region successfully resisted attempted interference by non-resident nobles. On the other hand lairds could use outside support,
such as influence at court, to their advantage. Royal offices and
commissions could increase a landed family's authority in their
locality but this could disrupt the balance of power in an area. It
was dangerous for a magnate to neglect the court as this gave
enemies a chance to ruin his reputation with the king. Local
power and influence at the centre reinforced each other.

Decentralisation was also inherent in the Scottish legal system.
Much of the law of early-modern Scotland had evolved from
within communities, tailor-made to fit their needs, rather than
being imposed from above. Central institutions like Parliament
served more to clarify and systematise the customs of communities rather than to impose a centralised code upon them
(Goodare, 1989). Much of the administration of justice was in the
hands of local landowners through a mosaic of franchise courts,
heritable jurisdictions of barony and regality within which the
interpretation of justice depended upon local custom. In
Roxburgh and Berwickshire, for instance, there were 58 heritable
jurisdictions: 3 regalities and 55 baronies (Meikle, 1988). The
large number of heritable jurisdictions gave lairds a greater
degree of involvement in local administration than landowners
on the English side of the Border.

Baronies were often small, local-scale units, although some
were large and fragmented. In many smaller baronies the
landowner was resident. Where he was an absentee, the administration of the baron court was left in charge of a baillie who

might range in status from a tenant farmer to a substantial laird depending on the size and importance of the barony. There may have been over 1,000 baronies in Scotland – more than the number of parishes – although no one has so far tried to enumerate them, far less map them. Baronies could deal with cases of theft where a criminal was caught in the act or with stolen goods in their possession, and with 'red handed' cases of slaughter as well as more minor assaults. Some baronies had the power of 'pit and gallows', the right to imprison and execute offenders. Even in the sixteenth century, however, there was often a considerable difference between the theoretical power of the baron courts and the offences they actually handled. The activities of many of them were mainly concerned with pursuing petty debts, maintaining 'good neighbourhood' among tenants and cottars, and ensuring that rents were paid and that feudal obligations and services were discharged.

Regalities were much more powerful judicial units. There may have been around 200 of them covering, according to some estimates, up to half of Scotland. They could try all but a few serious offences so that, in effect, they were petty kingdoms outside the jurisdiction of central authority. Some regalities were fairly small but some, like Atholl or Argyll, covered huge blocks of territory. Large regalities like Dunfermline and Orkney had administrative structures modelled on the royal courts, with justiciary courts trying capital offences and even going on circuit. Regality courts could try the 'four pleas of the crown': robbery, rape, murder and arson. Only treason and, after 1597, witchcraft lay outside their jurisdiction. The agents of the crown in the shires were the sheriffs. Although sheriffs were notionally royal officials, by the sixteenth century most of the offices had become hereditary and were in the hands of local families. Sheriff courts had comparable criminal jurisdictions to regalities, serving as courts of appeal for baronies.

English commentators on the Scottish judicial system were amazed at the hereditary character of the franchises and the extent of their powers. It has been customary to write off the Scottish system of heritable sheriffdoms, regalities and baronies as ineffective compared with the more sophisticated centralised system of justice in England (Davies, 1980). The granting away of rights on this scale has been seen as a sign of weakness on the part of Scottish monarchs. Under the Scottish system, however, local disputes and problems were dealt with by local people who, if they were amateur judges, at least understood local conditions and circumstances. The system retained a flexible, commonsense approach, which may have worked as well in its way as more complex structures. The devolution of administrative and judicial functions can be seen as encouraging responsibility, giving more landowners an opportunity to participate directly in the running of their localities than in England. It was an effective way of ensuring that justice in some form was provided in more remote areas by the people who were best placed to exert control. The patchwork of jurisdictions may seem confusing and inefficient but the various courts seem to have integrated with each other reasonably well.

An indication of how lightly central authority affected the localities in Scotland is provided by the number of royal officials in relation to the total population. The sheriffs and their deputies numbered perhaps 75 in the later sixteenth century against 1,738 English Justices of the Peace in 1580. This represents one local administrator for *c*.2,300 people in England against one per 13,000 in Scotland. France had one crown official for every 4,500 people in the early sixteenth century (Goodare, 1989). The contrast is reduced when it is appreciated that in Scotland officials were virtually all confined to the Lowlands. On the other hand this means that the third or more of the population living in the Highlands had no local royal officials at all. In England the number of Justices of the Peace increased faster than the overall population in the sixteenth century; in Scotland numbers of officials remained fixed while population rose.

Why was Scottish society so devolved with so much power in the hands of nobles and lairds? Until recently historians had no doubt that the problem lay with over-mighty magnates and a weak, ineffective crown. In the last two decades there has been a major revision of ideas regarding the nature of the relationship between crown and magnates in late-medieval Scotland, suggesting that it was generally based on co-operation and consensus rather than confrontation and conflict. Crown and nobility normally worked together in a responsible partnership (Wormald, 1981).

This approach has in turn led to a reappraisal of Scottish institutions as being different from those of neighbouring countries rather than simply primitive. Instead of lack of money preventing the development of complex institutions, lack of expensive central institutions reduced the need for Scottish monarchs to raise money to run them. The judicial system virtually financed itself and Scottish kings, still relying on the medieval concept of the 'common army' raised by sheriffs, did not need to employ paid mercenaries. The result was that Scotland was taxed infrequently and lightly compared with England and so a sophisticated and expensive money-gathering bureaucracy was not needed. This explains why monarchs like James IV, James V and Mary were able to live within their means despite a small income compared with English kings and even, in the case of the first two, indulge in ambitious building projects. Because the Scottish Parliament did not have responsibility for raising taxes very often this did not mean that it was weaker than the English House of Commons, only that its role was different. Decentralised *laissez-faire* rule is now seen as a deliberate royal policy as much as *faute de mieux*.

The Scottish parliament has been portrayed as primitive, moribund and ineffectual. Because parliamentary statutes were often repeated regularly it has been assumed that this indicated that they were being ignored. Goodare's (1989) study of late sixteenth-century Scottish parliaments has shown that this is a misleadingly simple interpretation. Sixteenth-century statutes tended to exaggerate the scale and seriousness of problems out of common form. They did not normally aim at full and permanent implementation despite their wording. Most legislation was permissive, encouraging local administrators to consider whether there was, in fact, a problem and providing them with a statutory framework if they decided that something needed to be done. The Poor Law act of 1575, for instance, was probably not implemented fully and immediately anywhere but it did give parishes a mechanism that they could use to cope with crises.

Feud and Faction

During the sixteenth century new pressures on society encouraged an increasing degree of centralisation of administration and justice. Political instability, population growth, inflation and changing patterns of landownership affected Scottish society in ways which have yet to be clearly established. Perhaps the most dramatic example of growing central control allied to major social change was the decline in feuding at the end of the sixteenth century. Bloodfeud was a long-established institution, which, despite the name, was not necessarily always violent or uncontrollable. Brown (1986) and Wormald (1981) have shown that feuds were at once more widespread in late sixteenth-century Scotland and, at the same time, less violent than has often been believed. They were by no means confined to the Borders and the Highlands but occurred throughout Scotland. At the late sixteenth-century peak there may have been at least 50 feuds in progress in Scotland at any time.

Bloodfeud involved private, kin-based justice where a murderer offered compensation to the kin and friends of the man he had killed. Private settlement of feuds with the help of kinsmen, friends and neighbours was often faster and fairer than going to law and it offered a realistic way of restoring peace in the localities. A man who lost out in a settlement was more likely to accept a ruling against him by his peers rather than a distant, anonymous court. Feuds were started for a variety of reasons but disputes over land ownership were an increasingly common one. In an honour society the establishment of peace in a feud was a slow and often difficult business; no one wanted to be seen to give concessions too easily. The initiative often came from kin, friends and neighbours. The use of lordship was an effective way of bringing about the settlement of a feud because any man who ignored a peace negotiated by his lord would find himself without support. A lord might intervene in the feud of a vassal but a lord in turn could be pressured by his own supporters.

The process of assythment, or agreed arbitration using mediators chosen by each party, was often resorted to in preference to pursuit before the law. It usually involved compensation in cash on a carefully graded scale that took in the nature of the crime, the wealth and status of killer and victim, and the size of the victim's family. A settlement following a murder was often easier to achieve because there was a mutual interest in preventing further violence while in a dispute over land there was a clear winner and a loser. A homage ceremony, representing a public humiliation for the killer, restored honour to the victim's family and compensated for their failure to exact blood vengeance. A feud might appear to have been settled but in circumstances where the same families lived in the same localities memories were long and new events could fan a feud into flame again. The nature of feudal power encouraged this; nobles and lairds needed to adopt an aggressive, competitive attitude merely to protect their existing interests. To refuse to compete was to invite your neighbours to walk all over you and to lose your supporters (Brown, 1986).

Feuding does not seem to have been as serious a problem in the fifteenth and early sixteenth centuries as in later decades. The background conditions of political instability and a range of social pressures, including increased competition for land once church and crown estates had been feued out, caused the number of feuds to increase greatly. Almost every noble and a great many lairds were involved in at least one feud. Feuds could have a severe impact on society at a local and even a regional level, as with the MacDonald/MacLean feud at the end of the sixteenth century, which devastated extensive areas of Kintyre.

Consideration of feuding leads on to a more general question: how violent was Scottish society in the sixteenth century? The traditional view, still current in popular histories, is that Scottish society was uniquely and intolerably violent. It has been suggested that the carrying of arms was virtually universal, with handguns becoming increasingly popular so that every tense encounter was a potential murder or manslaughter. The apparent frequency of feuding between landed families has been taken to indicate that violence was endemic at all levels of Scottish society. English observers certainly considered late sixteenth-century Scotland a violent place but they conveniently ignored the fact that feuding was also widespread in northern England too. More recently it has been pointed out that certain types of violence and protest, such as peasant uprisings, found in England and on the Continent, were rare in Scotland (Grant, 1984).

Feuding was only one type of violence and it is far from clear that the rise in feuding in the later sixteenth century was accompanied by the rise of other forms. In a society that, one might have thought, was hardened to violence some crimes still had the power to shock. In 1588 John Dickson, the son of a Border laird, outraged public opinion by murdering his father. He was forfeited and executed by being broken on the wheel (Meikle, 1988). In 1600 Jean Livingstone was sentenced to death. The daughter of a laird, she was trapped in an unhappy marriage with a violent man she did not love. She conspired with some of her servants to have him murdered. The disgust with which her crime was viewed is reflected in the fact that she was sentenced to be hanged and her body burnt, despite her status. The sentence was changed to beheading but her nurse, who was thought to have been an accomplice, and two other servants whose only crime was being in the wrong place at the wrong time, were burnt, probably after strangulation (Brown, 1992). The prominence of feuding may give a misleading impression and does not necessarily mean that other types of violence were particularly common or acceptable.

Nevertheless, levels of feuding did rise sharply in the 1570s, more slowly in the 1580s and peaked in the 1590s, creating a situation that was seen as intolerable by James VI, the church and even a growing section of the nobility. James in particular had a jaundiced view of the honour code of the nobility. He condemned the 'fectlesse arogant conceit of their greatnes and power; drinking in with their very nourish-milk, that their honour stood in committing three points of iniquitie: to thrall by oppression, the meaner sort that dwelleth neare them: to maintaine their servants and dependars in any wrong... and for anie displeasure, that they apprehend to be done unto them by their neighbours, to tak up a plaine feid [feud] against him, and, without respect to God, king or commonweale, to bang it out bravely, hee and all his kinne, against him and all his'.

By the later 1590s, however, James was in a stronger position to tackle the problem with the defeat of the earls of Huntly and Bothwell. He also had an ally in the church. As early as 1576 the General Assembly had condemned feuding but the kirk's attack intensified in the 1580s and 90s. In 1590 the king told the General Assembly that they had a mutual interest in promoting peace. An act of 1595 to pacify feuds gave presbyteries a role in the peace-making process. The greatest achievement of the church was not direct intervention in feuds but through influencing the general climate of opinion. Ministers were critical of the king for not taking a sufficiently firm approach to the problem and of the government and nobility for setting a bad example by not performing their role as godly magistrates. This was part of a broader attack by the kirk on kinship and its ramifications, including private justice. 'Let no thief pass because he is your servent, nor the murderer because he is your kinsman', thundered Robert Bruce, one of the most outspoken ministers.

The sustained campaign by the church brought the political community to face the problem and encouraged the nobles in Parliament and the Privy Council to join in a campaign to curb feuds. James disliked having the shortcomings of his government relentlessly exposed by the church but he agreed about the seriousness of the problem. With the English succession in view he wanted a united nobility behind him. The procession of feuding nobles hand in hand down the High Street of Edinburgh in 1587 as a token of friendship was largely a symbolic exercise but it was nevertheless an indication of increasing government strength that they agreed to do it at all.

In 1598 Parliament passed an act 'Anent Removing and Extinguishing Deidlie Feuds'. All parties at feud were to appear before James and the Privy Council so that arbitrators could be arranged. This approach was very conservative but it was remarkably successful, with many major feuds having been settled by 1603. Similar methods had been tried before and it can only be concluded that on this occasion it was reinforced by a major change of opinion among the nobility, how they thought about their world and the place of violence in it, how they could cope with rivals and enemies without resorting to violence. Many of the new nobility had been trained in law and set their face against traditional attitudes.

The kirk's initiative and new legislation were only two of the factors that brought about a rapid decline in feuding at the end of the sixteenth century, just as the reduction of feuding was only one element in a major change in the relationships between centre and locality. The idea that feuding was uncivilised was gaining ground and it was admitted to be a national embarassment. The idea of honour was being re-evaluated in Scotland, although identification of it with gentlemanly conduct and service to the state was slower to be accepted than in England. After 1603 the desire to counter the image of Scotland as a backward society had a major impact on the thinking of the Scots nobility. James continued to direct measures to curb feuding after 1603 but the problem was already in decline by then, due to a change of attitudes by the nobility as much as to royal policy.

The decline of feuding was also influenced by the increasing professionalism and centralisation of the legal system. The transition from locally administered customary law to centrally administered professional law had begun in the fifteenth century but accelerated in the late sixteenth. Central justice was slow, partial and favoured the powerful while the integrity of judges and lawyers was often compromised by their kinship links. Nevertheless, growing confidence in the legal system is suggested by the rise of litigation. As the legal system became more professionalised lawyers began to reject old amateur forms of justice. For example, the use of bonds of manrent ended quite abruptly in the early seventeenth century (Wormald, 1985).

Four decades of peace also helped to influence the nobility to end feuding, which declined steadily after 1600. Although the principles of private justice and assythment continued to be recognised by the courts into the 1640s, feuding had been driven from the Lowlands by the time of James' death in 1625. The attack on private violence, confining feuding to the more remote areas of the Highlands, was one of James VI's greatest achievements.

Pacifying the Borders

Sixteenth-century Scotland contained two 'problem regions', the Highlands and the Borders, over which central government had particular difficulty maintaining law and order. The problems posed by the Highlands will be considered in Chapter 5. It is important to emphasise that the problems of controlling these two regions were not the same. The Borders were close to an alien, sometimes hostile administration and faced recurrent war. The Highlands were distant and culturally distinctive. The Borders were heavily governed by Scottish standards for there was the additional apparatus of the wardenships. Because of this, and because of central government's close interest in Border affairs, the area was scrutinised closely and violence was well recorded. This may give the impression that the Borders were more lawless than they actually were. The Highlands, on the other hand, were under-governed, often barely governed at all. The only element of control was the system of granting powers of lieutenancy to favoured magnates and getting them to use their own armed followings to deal with recalcitrant clans and chiefs. This was, effectively, official sanction for private warfare, and it continued into the later seventeenth century. The amount of royal control over lieutenants was limited, the potential for abuse considerable. This mechanism was only used periodically, unlike the Borders where the wardenships were permanent features, their holders appointed direct by the crown and not hereditary. While the Borders had a long history of government interest it was only in the 1580s that the authorities started to pay attention to the Highlands.

The context of Border violence has been the subject of a good deal of debate. The social structure and economy of the region differed in degree rather than kind from the rest of the Lowlands. Yet the area, especially the Middle and West Marches, had unique problems as an upland pastoral region with a scattered population, uncomfortably close to a sometimes hostile frontier: classic bandit country. The endemic raiding and cattle rustling that continued to the end of the sixteenth century has been attributed to the destabilizing effect of periodic warfare with England. Until the mid-sixteenth century this region was always the first to be devastated in wartime. 'Peacetime' raiding has been seen simply as a continuation of warfare against the 'auld enemy' by other means. Certainly war damage caused poverty, which in turn increased the propensity of the inhabitants to restore their fortunes by cattle raiding rather than raising. It is often forgotten, however, that much of the reiving was by Scot against Scot while alliances between families often spanned the Border. Nor does this explain why, during the second half of the sixteenth century, when relationships between Scotland and England were generally peaceful, crime and violence on the Border should have persisted. The nature of the area, with its limited prospects for arable farming and its pastoral orientation, reinforced poverty and encouraged raiding. It is possible that the Borders were overpopulated in the sixteenth century, with pressure on available resources forcing Borderers into crime in order to survive. It has been suggested that Border families encouraged excessive subdivison of holdings in order to retain a numerous tenantry ready for war. Although partible inheritance and holding subdivision is known to have been wide-spread in parts of the English Borders, clear evidence of subdivision and overpopulation has yet to be presented for Scotland.

Popular accounts of Border society, from Sir Walter Scott's 'Lay of the Last Minstrel' onwards, highlight the most violent stories, often overlooking the fact that there was a significant diminution in the amount of raiding and violence in the later sixteenth century (Fraser, 1971). The fact that the authorities in Edinburgh kept a close eye on the region meant that the violence that did occur was more carefully scrutinised than in other areas, possibly providing a misleading picture. Feuds were a feature of Border society, some of them spectacularly violent, like the one between the Maxwells and Johnstones on the Western March. At its peak it assumed the proportions of a regional civil war. Its origins remain obscure but were undoubtedly linked to the rivalry of the two families for local supremacy. In 1585 Lord Maxwell raided John-stone lands in Annandale with 1,700 men and cut a swathe of destruction across the countryside. In 1593 Maxwell, in command of a force of around 2,000, was ambushed near Lockerbie by a smaller band of Johnstones. Maxwell was killed in the pitched battle that ensued and estimates of casualties on his side run as high as 700.

Attempts to maintain law and order on the Borders used an additional level of administration, the wardens of the three Marches. Rather than being high-profile military leaders their duties were, by the later sixteenth century, becoming more like routine police work. Although they often remained in the hands of powerful local families the wardenships did not become hered-itary like sheriffdoms. Being prominent local men meant, however, that the wardens also had their own interests to pursue. In the mid-sixteenth century the additional office of Keeper of Liddesdale developed in an attempt to control this particularly turbulent area. International incidents were dealt with by formal meetings of Scottish wardens with their English counterparts at days of truce. Much of the business at these meetings involved damage claims resulting from raids. Wardens also had extensive powers relating to internal as well as cross-Border affairs. These grew in the sixteenth century as they acquired a justiciary role enabling them to try cases of murder, slaughter, rape, arson, theft and even witchcraft.

Attempts to maintain law and order in the Borders involved the use of 'general bands' subscribed by heads of leading families who promised to maintain peace on behalf of their kinsmen and followers and to deliver to justice any law breakers. Alternatively, hostages were taken to ensure obedience. Prominent members of particular families were required to surrender themselves to royal authority and were lodged under open arrest in a royal castle or, more commonly, in the home of a prominent landowning family far from the Borders.

These measures were supplemented by periodic judicial raids from Edinburgh by monarch or regent. The expedition led by James V, when the famous outlaw Johnnie Armstrong was induced to submit to the king and was then promptly hanged, has become enshrined in folk history. This was, however, only one of many raids designed to demonstrate that the area did not lie beyond the reach of royal authority. Both judicial and punitive elements were involved. A circuit court would be established at a royal burgh like Dumfries or Jedburgh. Because the crown had to be seen to be successful in holding these special courts the cases that were considered were mainly ones in which convictions were fairly certain. There were few acquittals, hence the expression 'Jeddart (Jedburgh) justice': hang first, ask questions later. Criminals might, however, gain remission by admitting their guilt and offering to pay compensation. Local leaders would be brought in to sign general bands or deliver hostages as pledges of good conduct.

Some parts of the Borders, notably Eskdale and Liddesdale, were too remote and intractable for this to work. The military side of government expeditions involved raising local shire levies and devastating the lands of those who had not appeared to answer charges, or to subscribe to a general band. These raids were generally carried out after harvest, partly to ensure that the shire levies would turn up and partly to deprive the thieves of their food supply for the winter. Such actions might cause the reivers to lie low for a spell but by depriving them of their crops and livestock they guaranteed further raiding in the future.

Border society in the sixteenth century has been seen as distinctly different from the rest of Lowland Scotland. Border families or kinship groups, identified by their surnames, have been considered as analogous to Highland clans. As in the Highlands such family groups were not survivals from an ancient tribal system. They emerged in the Borders during the fourteenth and fifteenth centuries as a result of the insecurity created by English invasions. Their formation was encouraged by the geography of the region whose isolated valleys reinforced local solidarity. Family groups in these areas were sometimes described by contemporaries as clans but the temptation to see Border families as different from the rest of Lowland society should be resisted. As was the case elsewhere in the Lowlands kinship powerfully reinforced the feudal structure of society. The two systems were combined by members of prominent Border families to build up social and political power. Bonds of manrent were used to attach the support of men who were not related, producing large confederations like the one built up on the western Borders by the Maxwells early in the sixteenth century. Reivers ranged in social status from cottars and tenants to major landowners. Few were permanent outlaws, a term that was confined to small groups of 'broken men', often fugitives from justice from more settled parts of the Lowlands, who found shelter in the Debateable Land and other lawless districts.

During the sixteenth century the government increasingly intervened in the maintenance of law and order on the Borders. When justice was seen to be unobtainable locally due to the existence of powerful factions, individuals appealed direct to the Privy Council. The growth in the Council's volume of business relating to the Borders is reflected in 1590 by the setting up of a special committee to deal with Border affairs. Focusing on isolated raids, like Scott of Buccleuch's daring attack on Carlisle Castle in 1596 to rescue the notorious reiver Kinmont Willie, tends to hide the fact that by the later sixteenth century the Borders were more stable than in earlier decades. The last large-scale Border raid occurred in 1587 when around 2,000 Scots crossed into England as a reprisal for an English raid. Significantly, the leaders, Scott of Buccleuch and Ker of Cessford, were warded by order of the Scottish Privy Council. Efforts to channel feuds towards the law and growing day-to-day intervention by central government were having increasing success in defusing tension.

After the Union of 1603 the Border became an internal rather than an international problem. The Anglo-Scottish Border counties became the 'Middle Shires'. Concerted action by a series of special Border Commissions stamped out raiding. The old way of life ended rapidly once reivers could no longer play the authorities of two countries off against each other. After 1605 troops of horsemen patrolled the Border to prevent fugitives fleeing from one country to another. Some Borderers went abroad as mercenaries and effective policing of the area, combined with harsh summary justice, brought a rapid end to raiding and violence. Executions, restrictions on carrying arms and owning saddle horses, and the burning of the tower houses of known thieves, pacified the area quickly. Symbolically, the iron yetts of tower houses belonging to the most prominent reiving families were ordered to be taken down and re-forged into ploughshares.

The Grahams of the Debateable Land were singled out for special treatment. They were systematically persecuted, executed, dispossessed and banished, some being transported to the Low Countries, others to Ireland. Five years after the Union the only Grahams living openly in the Debateable Land were the sick and the elderly; the able-bodied ones who had sneaked back were in hiding. By this time levels of crime and violence were probably not much worse than elsewhere in the Lowlands. The relaxation of pressure by the authorities after 1611 led to renewed trouble but on a small scale compared with pre-Union activity. There were outbreaks of theft, cattle rustling and disorder later in the century, notably during the Revolution, while after the Restoration religious discontent and the holding of illegal conventicles posed problems, but these difficulties were strictly short term and small scale.

The Expansion of Central Government

The success with which feuding was tackled was only one aspect of the growing power of central government, and its increasing willingness to interfere in the localities. This process has been seen as a revolution in government leading to Stewart absolutism and despotism. Lee (1959, 1980) has claimed that there was a deliberate plan, hatched by James VI and his chancellor, Maitland of Thirlestane, to undermine the power of the aristocracy indirectly by increasing the efficiency of central administration. Lee considers that Stewart despotism was hostile to the nobility and was deliberately created by Maitland to curb the magnates. In this view there was a clash between a reactionary, declining nobility and a progressive crown allied to middling groups. An alternative interpretation, put forward by Brown (1986) and Wormald (1981), proposes a powerful nobility co-operating with a powerful crown. According to this theory James' success in increasing his power lay more in winning the support of the nobility than in direct attacks on their power.

Although the campaign to reduce feuding attacked other methods used by the nobility to maintain their client networks, such as forcing less powerful neighbours to depend on them, and protecting criminal followers, James was not anti-noble. Emphasis on crown/nobility tensions has obscured the amount of co-operation between the two. What James did was to restore the balance between crown and nobility to something comparable to what had existed under James V, with the co-operation of the nobles. Although there was no 'revolution' in Scottish government in the late sixteenth century, there was a marked expansion of bureaucracy and many central institutions were remodelled. Neither church nor crown was prepared to respect the traditional sensitiveness of Scottish society in the localities. The construction of a nation state in which individuals participated in government directly rather than through kin or client networks began in the 1580s. The scale of the shift from locality to centre can, however, be exaggerated. Scotland still remained a very decentralised country in which much power remained in the hands of the magnates.

To intervene in the localities the king required local co-operation. Under James VI in the late sixteenth and early seventeenth centuries there was more government, especially more central government. Military action became the exclusive preserve of the state. The last magnate rebellion, by the Catholic earls, was in 1594. A wider range of social groups were brought into direct contact with the government. The lairds and the lawyers were two key social sectors whose members were drawn into closer relationship with the crown.

In the long period of peace down to 1638 society became less warlike, the rapid decline in violence suggesting that the franchise courts were co-operating with the central judiciary. Wapinschaws continued to be held periodically in the last two decades of the sixteenth century but were virtually abandoned thereafter due to lack of public interest. Bans on the carrying of handguns, especially pistols, seem to have had some effect. In 1617 the Register of Sasines was established, a central record of land transactions. Previous attempts to create such a register had foundered due to the opposition of sheriffs and localities and a proposed statute in 1592 had not been enacted.

Another centralising influence was the crown's growing need for money. In the later sixteenth and early seventeenth century taxation became more frequent and much heavier, affecting a wider range of people and activities. Although the landed classes were forced to pay more it was the merchants of the royal burghs who bore the heaviest burden. Parliamentary taxation changed from being an occasional supplement to crown finances to being the mainstay of its income. This was partly due to a substantial reduction in the extent of crown lands. These had reached their maximum around 1542 but were rapidly feued out in the later sixteenth century to raise ready cash. This removed a major direct source of revenue to the crown and also reduced scope for patronage. The crown ceased, in effect, to be a feudal landlord. At the same time, despite inflation, income from the customs did not increase significantly.

The taxation system, which has been described by Goodare (1989) as a 'crazily patched structure', had been inherited from a low-pressure fiscal tradition and was now forced to cope with a high-pressure regime. Its effectiveness was reduced by the use of an outdated medieval assessment system. Valuations in Old Extent, dating from the Wars of Independence, had remained fixed while land values had not. By the sixteenth century they were often unrelated to people's ability to pay. The tax system was also slow to adapt to social changes and new sources of wealth. Among landowners only tenants in chief holding direct from the king were liable to pay. It was 1581 before feudal superiors were given authorisation to try and recoup some of the taxation from their feuars. Feuars only had to pay tax directly from 1597. Ministers' stipends remained untaxed during the sixteenth century and lawyers were not taxed until the 1630s. Despite this taxation rose rapidly. The highest tax under Regent Morton in the 1570s had been £12,000. In 1581 £40,000 was demanded, in 1588 £100,000 and in 1601 over £300,000. Drastic revision of customs rates and the introduction of duties on imports occurred in 1597 (Goodare, 1989).

Sensibly, James VI did not attempt to interfere with the heritable jurisdictions of the nobility. Nevertheless, he tried to alter the balance between centre and locality by establishing a new tier of administration. Commissioners of the Peace were launched in 1609 to improve law enforcement in the localities. They were not due solely to James' experience of England as there were precedents for them stretching back to 1581. The term 'Justice' was carefully avoided, although their powers were similar to English Justices of the Peace in many respects. They were designed to replace sheriffs and their main job was to keep the peace but they had little authority over the landed gentry and almost none over the nobles. They were supposed to deal with minor disturbances, enforce laws on vagrancy and deal with weights and measures, wages and prices, and the repair of roads and bridges. They were also authorised to appoint constables under them, at least two in every parish. The new officials were not popular and there was a lack of co-operation from sheriffs or magistrates. It was difficult for them to find a slot for their jurisdiction among the networks of franchises but they were not entirely ineffective, providing an additional layer of authority at a local level. Due to hostility from barons and lords of regality they were relaunched in 1612 as a supplement, rather than an alternative, to the heritable jurisdictions.

Prior to efforts to introduce constables responsible to the new Commissioners there were no officials at parish level, except in the Northern Isles where they were a survival from the Norse administrative system. The new constables met with little success: it is doubtful whether they were even appointed in most parishes. During the later sixteenth and early seventeenth centuries community life was transformed by the development of a new, powerful and effective system of centralised control, the kirk sessions (Chapter 3). Since the Reformation the parish had grown more significant as a focus for communities at the expense of the barony. The church had developed a far more effective system of local government, led by its professionally trained ministers, than the state. The network of kirk sessions and, later, presbyteries, represented a formidable mechanism for social control.

Despite the strength of kirk sessions, centre and locality were nevertheless often only loosely linked in the early seventeenth century. The outbreak of the Covenanting wars in 1638 led to a much greater integration of the two as a result of the pressure to raise men and money. In 1638 the last major war in Scotland had been 60 years earlier. Few wapinschaws or musters had been held after 1603. Their military significance was limited, even in towns like Edinburgh where they were held relatively frequently, unlike London whose trained bands formed the nucleus of the Parliamentary army in 1642.

From the very start of the Covenanting period people in the localities were much more closely involved in national politics than ever before. This is shown by the way in which copies of the National Covenant were sent round every burgh and parish to be signed by the bulk of the adult male population. Under pressure of war the Covenanters achieved a thorough reorganisation of Scottish government, with the development of a centralised administration which ensured that directions from Edinburgh were uniformly carried out in the localities. Committees of war were set up in each sheriffdom to raise, train, equip and provision regiments. The system of raising a national conscript army was derived from Sweden, where Alexander Leslie, commanding the Covenanting army, had been a field marshal. Numbers of men required for the army were determined for each parish and burgh. Fencible men were listed by ministers and elders and selection was made by each community. Between 1639 and 1651 the Covenanters raised over a dozen armies, some with up to 24,000 men. The level of recruitment was not much below that of Sweden, a much more militarised and wealthy society, with up to 3 per cent of the total population serving in the army in 1644 (Furgol, 1990).

As well as men the Covenanting administration needed money on a scale hitherto unseen in Scotland to equip, train and maintain them. Early in 1640 nobles, lairds and heritors in each presbytery were required to choose landed men who could determine the incomes of landowners in each parish. The first national tax by the Covenanters, a tenth of valued rents, was designed to be more equitable than the previous system, taxing all landholders and not just tenants in chief. Moreover, the tax was not just on land but on all income. Eighty-four per cent of the tax was actually paid, quite an achievement. The amounts raised by the Covenanters were greater than any previous taxation. The use of valued rents as the basis for taxation was retained after the Restoration. Demands for men, money and commitment politicised the people throughout Scotland during the Scottish Revolution. Operating primarily through the church hierarchy and local landowners, the power of the state must for the first time have seemed stronger to ordinary people than that of their landlords.

The Cromwellian occupation brought even tighter control of local administration, especially justice, and showed that no part of Scotland was immune from central interference. In 1652 the heritable jurisdictions were abolished. Justices of the Peace were re-established in 1656 but the Cromwellian administration could not find any better means of social control than the existing kirk sessions, so they retained them. Passes were required for people to move about and the carrying of firearms was restricted. This was a military occupation by an army of over 10,000, dispersed in strategically located garrisons including Inverness and Inverlochy. By 1655 it was claimed that 'a man may ride all over Scotland with £100 in his pocket, which he could not have done these 500 years'. Taxation to maintain the occupying forces was over five times that of Charles I's reign.

The upset and dislocation caused by the Covenanting wars and Cromwellian occupation have been viewed more in terms of their impact on Scotland's economy rather than society. In social terms the period has often been viewed as an isolated, aberrant phase. It is difficult to believe, however, that there was not a longer-term, destabilising effect on late seventeenth-century society. For one thing society had been thoroughly militarised. After the long period of peace down to 1638 and the laws against the use of handguns, it is likely that carrying arms had greatly diminished. Certainly, massive imports of weapons from the Netherlands were needed to equip the first Covenanting armies. By the 1650s Scotland must have been flooded with firearms and other weapons and, despite the ban on carrying weapons enforced by the Cromwellian regime, many of them must have remained in people's possession. If 6 per cent or more of the total male population was serving in the Covenanting armies in any year during the 1640s the proportion of men in the Lowlands who received military training at some point must have been far higher. The knock-on effects of this after 1660 can perhaps be seen in the readiness of western Covenanters to hold armed conventicles, to engage in virtual guerilla war with the authorities and, on occasion, successfully to challenge government forces in pitched battle, as at Drumclog in 1679. The militarisation of society in the 1640s, as well as a growing split between the nobility and greater gentry on one hand and an increasingly radical element of the ordinary population on the other, may have encouraged the first truly popular armed rebellion in Scotland, the Whiggamore Raid of September 1648, in which 2,000 Covenanters from the south west marched on Edinburgh and installed the radical Kirk Party (Makey, 1979). Another effect of mid-century political conditions, discussed more fully in Chapter 5, was to draw the inhabitants of the Highlands out of their isolation to have a significant effect on British, not just Scottish, politics.

Law and Order, Crime and Violence in Late Seventeenth- and Early Eighteenth-century Scotland

In administrative terms efforts to strengthen government influence over the localities continued after 1660. The heritable jurisdictions were restored but the central authorities had inherited new tools from the Covenanting and Cromwellian regimes. People had become used to paying higher taxes. The rate that Parliament approved for Charles II – £40,000 a year – was almost

three times that of the 1620s. The Cromwellian monthly maintenance land tax was retained as the cess. This tax needed a new
group of officials to collect it, the Commissioners of Supply. Their
qualification was the ownership of land worth £100 rent a year, a
fairly modest sum, regardless of the nature of its tenure. The
Commissioners of Supply, based on the Covenanters' shire
committees for war, led to the emergence of a weak 'shire community', giving the gentry a sense of corporate identify and encouraging them to become more dominant locally.

Covenanting rebellions aside, Lowland society in the later
seventeenth and early eighteenth centuries seems to have been
fairly peaceable. Baron court books for this period show only
occasional cases of minor assault of a kind suggestive of small-scale
quarrels that got out of hand rather than a high level of endemic
brutality and violence. In many sets of court records there is a
decrease in the number of cases involving violence as one moves
from the seventeenth into the eighteenth century. While some of
this may have been due to the atrophying of the franchise courts,
the shift to a more peaceful society was marked in the landscape,
outside the Highlands, by the end of the construction of fortified
houses and their remodelling on more spacious, comfortable
lines, along with the construction of new, undefended mansions.
There was, by the early eighteenth century, a distinct difference in
levels of violence between the Highlands and the Lowlands, highlighted by Leneman's (1986) observation on the kirk session
records of the Lowland parish of Fossoway and the Highland one
of Blair, both on the Atholl estates. In the former the most
frequent case of Sabbath breaking was drunkenness, in the latter
getting involved in a brawl. Carrying weapons remained common
on the margins of the Highlands into the eighteenth century.
Even in the early eighteenth century it was still common for
people – not just the nobility – to wear swords in the street, while
picking a fight with Edinburgh's town guard was a popular holiday
recreation (Houston, 1994). Nevertheless, there are no indications that society in Lowland Scotland at this time tolerated high
levels of violence.

Lowland society in the later seventeenth and early eighteenth
century thus appears as stable, almost subservient, compared with
that of England or Ireland. This has been attributed to the

control exerted by landowners and kirk sessions, and the strength of vertical linkages in Scottish society. While levels of popular protest seem to have been lower than in England, it nevertheless existed. The activities of the Covenanters in the 1660s, 70s and 80s, the violent eviction of ministers by local mobs in 1688, and disputes over church patronage from the 1730s, show that protest often had a religious focus (Chapter 3). In addition baron court books provide evidence of what could be interpreted as smaller scale acts of protest: breaking dykes, cutting green wood, assaulting barony officers and accumulating rent arrears when the harvest had been good (Whatley, 1990).

There was also a tradition of urban protest and riot. After 1707 anti-Union or anti-English feeling caused problems. The most frequent cause of violence was the new customs and exise duties. These made smuggling more profitable and caused customs officials, many of them English, to be hated. Attacks on them were widespread and even with the backing of the military large stretches of the coast were, at times, beyond official control. With a stagnant economy sharp rises in the cost of basic commodities like ale and salt as a result of the new duties hit many people hard. Involvement in smuggling may have been due to sheer necessity rather than profiteering. Significantly, when economic conditions began to improve in the 1740s attacks on customs officials became less common.

Whatley (1990) has estimated that around 60 people were killed in Scotland in the 1720s and 30s as a result of mob violence associated directly or indirectly with taxation, a figure comparable to the number of deaths due to rural protest in Ireland between 1761 and 1790, traditionally seen as a far more violent country. Most of this violence was urban. The incidence of urban mob violence in Scotland has been played down by considering events like the lynching of the captain of the English ship Worcester in 1705, the malt tax riots in Glasgow in 1705 and the Porteous riots in Edinburgh in 1736 as isolated incidents rather than part of an established tradition of urban riot extending back at least into the sixteenth century.

Edinburgh experienced serious riots in 1664, 1672, 1678, 1682, 1688–91, 1706–7, 1736 and 1740. Houston (1994) has shown that riots in Edinburgh at this period were not a sign of division or a threat to social cohesion but, as in England, an accepted mechanism by which different elements in the community could interact, providing the young and non-burgess element of the population with an opportunity to express their views. The larger riots were broadly based protests focusing on problems generated from outside the city, such as religion, taxes or political changes. The ambivalent attitude of the authorities towards such riots suggests implicit recognition of the importance of street protest to urban society. Only from 1740 did riots become more sectional and lower class in character, the protests more markedly violent and related to standards of living.

A notable feature of Scottish society was the way in which the wholesale transformation of rural society, which generally accompanied the adoption of agricultural improvement on a large scale, was accomplished with very little unrest compared with the various crofters' wars in the Highlands in the nineteenth century. The only true agrarian protest was the Levellers' Revolt in Galloway in 1723–25. Gangs of tenants and cottars, protesting at the engrossment of holdings by landowners to create large cattle ranches, went round the area throwing down the walls of cattle parks and, in some cases, slaughtering the animals. The relatively sensitive handling of this disturbance by the government suggests that dispossession on this scale was seen at the time as undesirable. The roughly contemporary clearance of small tenants and cottars in the eastern Borders produced no comparable opposition. In the later eighteenth century Devine (1994) has shown that individuals and small groups of farmers were indeed opposed to improvement and social change, sometimes taking a truculent attitude by blocking landowners' efforts, but not in a violent manner.

* * *

The heritable jurisdictions were confirmed in 1707 as a measure to encourage the support of landowners for the Treaty of Union, although subsequent years saw growing infiltration by the central courts into the activities of the franchises. In the early eighteenth century the franchise courts continued to function. In regalities like Atholl and Montrose offenders were still being executed for theft in the 1730s (Leneman, 1986). Lowland regality courts also retained important commercial roles, regulating prices, wages and markets, even if some of them had let many of their judicial powers lapse. By the 1740s many regality courts were letting the High Court of Judiciary encroach on their criminal cases and were acting primarily as co-ordinating bodies for groups of baron courts. In 1747, in the aftermath of Culloden, regalities and heritable sherriff's offices were abolished. Baron courts were retained but their powers were curtailed. This was in flagrant breach of the Treaty of Union but the government, thoroughly shaken by the 1745 rebellion, was in no mood to compromise. While the Scottish legal system continued to retain its separate identity, one of its most distinctive features had finally been removed some 150 years after James VI had condemned it, allowing the Scottish legal system to move closer to that of England. John Wilkes, writing in 1763, claimed that 'the principal part of the Scottish nobility are tyrants and the whole of the common people are slaves'. Although exaggerated, his claim contains an element of truth, emphasising deep-rooted aspects of Scottish society and the role of social control within it.

5

HIGHLAND AND LOWLAND

In one sense the theme of Highland and Lowland is merely that of Centre and Locality writ large. In another the relation between the two major divisions of Scotland is a different question because of the cultural contrasts between them. The tendency to treat the Highlands separately is sometimes deplored by Scottish historians yet the fact remains that contemporaries perceived and treated the region and its inhabitants as different from the rest of the country.

For all that the Highlands have generated a remarkable volume of romantic and sentimental writing there is still a lack of basic research on many key historical issues. Partly this reflects the belief that documentary sources are inadequate to allow many important questions to be tackled, including fundamental themes like the origin and evolution of clans. Nevertheless, a recent study of the history of Clan MacGregor in the sixteenth century (MacGregor, 1989) has demonstrated that the available sources are indeed sufficient to allow much detailed work to be done. Another barrier to research, perhaps more fundamental, is the difficulty experienced by modern scholars in coming to grips with the nuances of past Celtic culture.

Highlander and Lowlander

In Scotland consciousness of the distinctiveness of the High-lands and its inhabitants seems to have developed by the mid-fourteenth century. John of Fordun, writing in the 1380s, was the first author to suggest that the Highlanders were socially and culturally inferior to the Lowlanders. His tone was echoed with varying shades of scorn and contempt for the next 350 years. Highlanders were seen as different in terms of their language, their military prowess and their lawlessness. There was an element of racism in Lowland views of their Highland neighbours; they saw them as alien, describing their language as 'Irish' rather than 'Gaelic'. Highlanders in turn saw Lowlanders as invaders and usurpers who had driven them from the fertile plains, a suitable pretext for raiding and driving off their cattle. Highland society perpetuated kin-based institutions like blood-feuds and bonds of manrent, which were fast disappearing from the Lowlands in the early seventeenth century. An element of the Lowlanders' derision of Highland society may have stemmed from the subconscious realisation that the Lowlands had only recently shed such patterns of behaviour.

To the Lowlander the Highlander was increasingly a figure of ridicule, tempered with menace. One of Alexander Montgomerie's sixteenth-century poems described how God created the first Highlander from a horse turd. Surveying his creation:

Quoth God to the Helandman quhair [where] wilt thou now?
I will doun to the Lawland, lord and thair steill a kow'.

A similar attitude is evident a century later in lines by the Covenanter poet William Cleland:

Their head, their neck, their legs and thighs
Are influenced by the skies,
Without a clout to interrupt them,
They need not strip them when they whip them,
Nor loose their doublet when they're hanged...
Naught like religion they retain,
Of moral honesty they're clean,
In nothing they're accounted sharp,
Except in bagpipe and in harp,
For a misobliging word,
She'll durk her neighbour ov'r the board.

Though hardly great verse the author manages to deride Highland dress, religion, culture and morals with remarkable economy. If Cleland's views seem extreme, it should be remembered that he met an untimely death, shot by a Highland Jacobite when leading his regiment in the defence of Dunkeld in 1689. His view of Highlanders had almost certainly been coloured by the episode of the Highland Host in 1678 when, due to a refusal of the gentry of the western Lowlands to accept a bond making them responsible for their tenants' religious misdeeds, the government quartered an army of 5,000 Highlanders on their estates for a few weeks. Although most of the Highlanders were drawn from southern and eastern areas, which had some contact with the Lowlands, stories about their barbarism, uncouth dress, language, manners and plundering lost nothing in the telling. Their poverty was shown by the things that they carried back home with them; shoes, tools and ironware – even coulters off ploughs. Lowlanders continued to refer to their Highland neighbours as 'aborigines' and 'savages' well into the eighteenth century.

Modern commentators would add that the clan system made Highland society distinctive but this did not strike Lowlanders during the sixteenth century as being significant. More recently, historians have tended to view contrasts in the society of the Highlands and Lowlands as ones of emphasis and chronology rather than of kind. The suggestion by Smout (1969) that Highland society was based on kinship modified by feudalism, Lowland society on feudalism modified by kinship, emphasises this. It is very easy, but also very misleading, to write of Highland society as if it were geographically uniform, especially in view of the lack of detailed local and regional studies. The balance between Celtic and feudal traditions varied within the Highlands, with a gradation from a more feudalised east and south towards the north and west. This distinction was recognised by James VI when he wrote that the Highlanders were divided into two groups, those of the mainland 'that are barbarous for the most parte yet mixed with some shewe of civilitie' and those living in the Isles who were 'totally barbarous'.

The division between Highland and Island has recently been emphasised by Dawson (1992). The medieval Lordship of the Isles was a seaborne empire embracing the Hebrides and the west coast mainland but not the interior of the Highlands. Its closest connexions were with Celtic Ireland. During the sixteenth century the linkages of this area began to be reoriented. The destruction of the Lordship of the Isles in 1493 reduced the split between mainland and island as mainland-based clans like the Campbells and Mackenzies extended their empires to embrace the Hebrides. Previous distinctions between the Western Isles and the Highlands faded out. Tudor policy in Ireland began to drive a wedge between Scottish and Irish branches of the MacDonalds. The plantation of Ulster by Lowland Scots in the early seventeenth century redirected the province's contacts to the Clyde and south west Scotland. There had long been a substantial coastal trade between the west Highlands and the Clyde; much of Glasgow's gradual rise in the late sixteenth and early seventeenth centuries was based on it. The growth of the cattle trade to the Lowlands and, later in the seventeenth century, to England encouraged the development of overland routes linking the Highlands to Lowland market centres. In the south west the expansion of the Campbells, with their efficient centralised organisation, tight control over cadet branches and increasing links with the Lowlands, strengthened contact across the Highland line.

Some Highland landowners were feudal magnates pure and simple, like the Murray earls and dukes of Atholl. There was no clan Murray; the inhabitants of the Atholl states were mainly Robertsons and Stewarts. The powers of the dukes of Atholl within their regality were no different from their Lowland counterparts; they were merely exercised in the context of a different society. It was the feudal tenure of wardholding that allowed Highland landowners to mobilise men for war in the Jacobite rebellions of 1715 and 1745. This explains why after Culloden the abolition of wardholding and heritable jurisdictions like regalities were the most important and far-reaching measures taken to curb the power of Highland clans.

The extent of the Gaidhealtachd, the area of Gaelic speech, provides a means of delimiting the Highlands as a cultural province between the early sixteenth and mid-eighteenth centuries (Withers, 1984). In the eleventh century Gaelic had been spoken as far south as the Tweed and Solway but the language retreated steadily from the Lowlands as English, spearheaded by Anglo-Norman landholders and their followers in the countryside and English-speaking burgesses in the towns, advanced. Gaelic may have survived in parts of lowland Aberdeenshire into the sixteenth century and in Galloway into the seventeenth but apart from these isolated pockets the boundary between Gaelic and English stabilised. It followed closely the topographic edge of the Highlands in the south. Parishes astride the Highland line, like Aberfoyle and Port of Menteith, contained distinct areas of English and Gaelic speech. English penetrated the Angus glens and the Dee valley but the intervening upland areas remained Gaelic-speaking. Inverness was a bilingual town and English maintained footholds further north in the Black Isle and eastern Caithness but otherwise all the inhabitants north of the Great Glen (excluding Orkney and Shetland) spoke Gaelic. Once the linguistic boundary had become fixed, Gaelic speech served to define the Highlander. Lowland dismissal of the language involved the rejection of a culture which, although orally based, was rich, especially in music and poetry.

The Highlands were far from being an isolated backwater. The very poverty of the area forced men to look elsewhere for a living. The region was an important source of mercenaries for wars in Ireland in the sixteenth century and on the continent in the seventeenth. It is also a mistake to assume that the Highlands were unaffected by central government during the sixteenth century. As well as deliberate government intervention the Highlands were influenced by the accidental, knock-on effects of royal policies, such as forfeitures, which created vacuums, destabilizing areas by encouraging surrounding clans to expand into them.

Changing Highland Society: The Sixteenth and Early Seventeenth Centuries

Despite all that has been written about Highland clans we still know remarkably little about how they evolved and functioned. They were not survivals of ancient Celtic tribalism but seem to have developed from the fourteenth century when the spread of feudalism into the Highlands was checked by the declining power of the monarchy. They arose from a need for local leaders to protect themselves and their followers without the support of central authority. Protection, as in sixteenth-century Lowland society, effectively meant aggressive expansion. The takeover of new lands by a clan could be legitimised by various means, including ones based on feudal authority or on kinship. Space does not permit a detailed discussion of the nature and evolution of clans but Dodgshon's (1989) approach, applying a model derived from anthropological theory, provides the most challenging recent reinterpretation.

The nature of the rise and fall of particular clans has been highlighted by a recent study of the MacGregors (MacGregor, 1989). The eponymous ancestor of the clan seems to have lived in the early fourteenth century and within three generations the clan name was established. Their ancestral lands in Glen Strae and Glen Orchy were absorbed by Campbell overlords in the late fourteenth century but the Campbells seem to have accepted the MacGregors as the established kindred in the area. For a century they were clients of the chiefs of Clan Campbell, later earls of Argyll and, from 1554, of a cadet branch, the Campbells of Glenorchy.

The later fifteenth and much of the sixteenth century saw a steady eastward expansion of Campbell influence, filling a vacuum created by James I's forfeiture of the Albany Stewarts. Under the Campbells the MacGregors also spread into western Perthshire, often spearheading the process of conquest and settlement. The MacGregors expanded at a lower level as tenants, their Campbell overlords as crown tenants in chief, fortified with commissions of lieutenancy and justiciary. This expansion created a number of separate new branches of the MacGregors in areas like Glen Lyon, Glen Lochay, Glen Dochart, Glen Lednock, Glen Gyle, Balquhidder and Strathyre, along with a tendency for the clan's identify to fragment. The rise of status and power of the MacGregors was reflected in the manipulation of their pedigree to claim more remote and illustrious ancestors.

In the first half of the sixteenth century there was a change in the relationship between overlord and client as the influence of the Campbells of Glenorchy declined and that of the MacGregors continued to grow, perhaps becoming in military terms the most important force in the area. After 1550 there was a revival in the fortunes of the Campbells of Glenorchy with a dramatic new phase of expansion under the dynamic influence of the sixth and seventh chiefs. A feeling that the MacGregors had become too strong and posed a potential threat may have contributed to a disastrous breakdown in relations with the Campbells, as may MacGregor hostility to the establishment of cadet branches of the chiefs of Glenorchy in MacGregor spheres of influence.

Although they had been useful in earlier phases of expansion, there was no longer a place in the Campbell scheme of things for a subordinate clan as powerful and independent as the MacGregors. This was typical of the process of clan expansion. What was unusual, and what ultimately led to the MacGregors being marginalised and singled out for special punitive treatment by the government, was the fact that they forcefully resisted Campbell pressure. The result was a bitter, violent feud between certain branches of the MacGregors and the chiefs of Glenorchy between 1562 and 1570.

The cause of the MacGregor/Campbell feud shows how, even in the sixteenth century, events in the Highlands were influenced, and to some degree directed, by central authority. The government backed the Campbells, issuing them with commissions of fire and sword against MacGregors over a wide area. The feud was affected by a power struggle at court when the Campbells lost the support of Mary Stewart. The Queen tried to win over the MacGregors, who were also by then being courted by the Campbells themselves, anxious for military assistance in mounting a rebellion against the crown. A fragile peace was restored in 1570 but by then extensive areas of western Perthshire had been devastated.

The MacGregors, now marginalised, became involved in other feuds and in endemic cattle raiding. They were identified in the popular mind as violent troublemakers. The chiefs of Glenorchy used legal means to try and eject them from their traditional lands in Glen Strae but the MacGregors held on tenaciously despite Campbell power and influence. When, in 1587, Parliament passed an act making Highland landlords responsible for any 'broken men' living on their lands the MacGregors headed the list of especially lawless clans. In 1603, two days before James left for London, he had the Privy Council proscribe the MacGregors as a reprisal for their attack on the Colquhouns in Glen Fruin earlier that year. In March of the following year 34 MacGregors were executed for their part in the battle. The MacGregors nevertheless survived into the eighteenth century. Their most notable characteristic in these later times was their conservative approach, clinging to traditions of feasting, feuding and raiding that were being abandoned by the clans around them, leaving them increasingly as misfits, social bandits in a changing society (Dodgshon, 1989).

The dramatic expansion of the Campbells in the sixteenth century and the MacGregors under them emphasises the degree of instability and unrest that existed in the Highlands following the destruction of the Lordship of the Isles by James IV in 1493. The Lordship had been, effectively, an independent state embracing the Hebrides and large areas of the west Highland mainland. Its removal and, more significantly, the failure of the crown to impose effective control on the west Highlands following its demise, led to a period of bitter feuding among the clans competing for power in the vacuum left by the downfall of the Lordship. Throughout the sixteenth century the crown sought to maintain some tenuous control over the area by appointing the leaders of powerful local families as royal lieutenants. The rise of the Campbells in the south west, the Gordons in the north east and the Mackenzies in the north reflects the aggrandisement that such positions allowed. The families selected as crown representatives had their own interests to pursue and often manipulated local events to their benefit, encouraging disorder among their neighbours and then stepping in to crush it and pick up the spoils.

The impact of the Reformation on the Highlands was limited and patchy at first. Under the enthusiastically protestant earls of Argyll the church made considerable headway in the south west but even by the mid-seventeenth century the church was still at a missionary stage over much of the region. Schemes to train Gaelic-speakers for the ministry in 1648 gathered momentum in 1650s but Highland parishes were huge and suitable ministers few. The kirk's apparatus for social control, including elders, kirk sessions and presbyteries, did not exist over much of the Highlands until well into the eighteenth century.

Despite the limited impact of central government the Highlands were not isolated from Lowland economic and social influences in the sixteenth century. There are, for instance, indications of more commercial attitudes by many clan chiefs towards their lands. The rise of the Campbells of Glenorchy has been attributed to wealth based on more efficient extraction of rents and casualties. There is also evidence in the late sixteenth century of growing financial pressures; indebtedness was responsible for the fall of some chiefs and the decline in the influence of others. Further aspects of Lowland influence can be seen in the restructuring by the Campbells of Glenorchy of their retinue to include non-Gaelic speaking Lowlanders as tutors, notaries and financial advisors, and early estate improvement including new castles, parks and plantations, as well as evidence of more efficient record keeping and estate administration (MacGregor, 1989). The late sixteenth-century chiefs of Glenorchy were clearly happy to introduce new ideas even if they went against tradition and customary ties. Gaelic culture continued but new radical elements of change were being introduced.

Nevertheless, for much of the sixteenth century central government impinged relatively lightly on the Highlands. While Lowland magnates tried to take over and manipulate central government Highland chiefs ignored it as far as possible, paying lip service to the idea of monarchy but preferring to focus on local issues rather than becoming involved in national politics. In return central government ignored the region unless its inhabitants affected the Lowlands. There can hardly be said to have been an official policy on the Highlands before the 1580s when James VI began to take a more active interest in the problems of law and order in the area. James' approach to the Highlands created a framework within which later governments continued to operate. In 1597 he ordered all chiefs to produce feudal charters for their lands and to be answerable for the behaviour of their inhabitants. He may have hoped to be able to forfeit lands held without written title and plant Lowland colonists on them. Recognising the difficulty of imposing direct central control on the region, James made the clans responsible for policing themselves, getting chiefs and landowners to subscribe to bands in which they agreed to answer for the conduct of their clansmen and tenants.

James' response to the problem of control in the Highlands was based on a violent unreasoning hatred for the 'uncivilised' Highlanders. He saw genocide as a prime solution with the extermination of the most lawless elements, the dispossession of chiefs and tacksmen and the plantation of Lowlanders. This may have been in part a reflection of Tudor policy in Ireland but he did not have resources on the same scale to make such a policy effective. The inability of the crown to mount major military expeditions to the Highlands made this a less realistic approach in Scotland. Colonising schemes in the Highlands worked best, if at all, when local help was involved, as with the settlement of Lowlanders in Kintyre under Campbell influence. Private ventures to colonise more distant areas did not succeed. In 1597 attempts were made by a group of Lowland entrepreneurs to colonise the island of Lewis. In 1605, and again in 1607–8, further efforts were made but the scheme was a total failure.

The Union of 1603 allowed concerted action against the operation of Highland mercenaries in Ireland and the Ulster plantations thrust a wedge between the two Gaelic areas. James' hatred of the Highlanders was tempered by the pragmatism of his Privy Council and it was due to this compromise that the Statutes of Iona were drawn up. In 1608 Lord Ochiltree, the king's lieutenant, led an expedition to the Isles. A group of prominent West Highland chiefs was tricked into capture. After imprisonment for some months they were forced to attend a conference on Iona in 1609 where they agreed to a range of proposals. Chiefs would be responsible for their clansmen and would appear regularly before the Privy Council in Edinburgh to account for their conduct. The Statutes and follow-up legislation in 1616 attempted to impose curbs on the chiefs' traditional lifestyle, including the size of their households, the number of war galleys they maintained, feasting and drinking, carrying firearms and exacting hospitality from their followers. Bards, troublemakers whose heroic poetry was liable to incite violence, were to be suppressed. Landowners in the Isles worth 60 cows or more were to have their eldest sons (in the 1616 act all their children) educated in the Lowlands and taught English.

The details of the Statutes show that the government had a clear idea of the role of feasting and feuding in the clan system (Dodgshon, 1989). By trying to limit conspicuous consumption and the maintenance of retainers they were endeavouring to undermine the ideology of the clan. Many of the stipulations were unenforcable but by making chiefs responsible for their men and bringing them to Edinburgh with some regularity the legislation increased contact between the leaders of Highland and Lowland society, developing in chiefs a desire for more ostentatious and expensive lifestyles. Despite the fact that the incomes of chiefs are likely to have risen with more settled conditions and the growth of the cattle trade many were soon in financial difficulties. Some chiefs had to raise large sums as sureties for their good behaviour or to meet fines imposed for the misdemeanors of their clansmen. Policing their territories, travel to the Lowlands, residence there and the fees of Edinburgh lawyers were additional drains on their resources.

The Statutes of Iona have been seen as a watershed marking the beginnings of effective government control over the Highlands but their significance has been exaggerated. They were one stage in a steady trend towards closer links between Highland and Lowland. Many of the changes that occurred during the seventeenth century, such as the gradual commutation of food renders to payments in cash, would have occurred whether the Statutes had been drawn up or not as the two regions slowly became more closely integrated economically and socially. The attempt to require chiefs to have their children educated in the Lowlands was an extension to the Hebrides of what was already an established trend on the Highland mainland. All ten chiefs who subscribed to the Statutes were sufficiently literate to sign their names.

The Statutes were designed to help re-orient West Highland chiefs towards Scotland rather than Ireland, forcing them to conform to the standards of the rest of Scotland's landowning classes. The change from food renders to money to support more expensive lifestyles for the chiefs was significant in eroding the ideology of clans, as were government efforts to encourage chiefs to grant written leases or tacks to their 'daoine uaisle' or gentry, a group that later became known as 'tacksmen' for this very reason. The commercialisation of the relationship between chief and tacksman, tacksman and clansman helped to undermine the traditional values of clanship. Although not all chiefs appeared before the Privy Council in every year in the later part of James' reign, there was a sufficient response to exert considerable influence on them. Under Charles I substantial sureties

encouraged more frequent appearances and compulsory attendance was enforced until 1638. The increased spending by chiefs
in meeting their obligations deepened their debts and in turn
encouraged the more commercial exploitation of their estates.

An increasing cultural gulf was opening by the mid-seventeenth century between the chiefs, with their broader outlook
and more expensive lifestyles, and their conservative clansmen.
This was expressed by the bards, champions of the old ways.
They increasingly criticised the extravagance of their chiefs and
their long stays in Edinburgh. Although the Statutes of Iona had
been directed more against itinerant bards than the established
bardic schools patronised by particular chiefs, there was a widespread breakdown of bardic patronage in the 1630s and 40s. A
rise of vernacular Gaelic poetry in a less constrained tradition
than that of the classical Gaelic bards was encouraged by
growing penetration of Lowland influences. Vernacular poetry
also condemned the negative aspects of closer involvement in
Lowland society (Macinnes, 1985).

The Highlands in a Wider Political World

As chiefs became increasingly assimilated into the rest of the
Scottish landowning class they began to be involved in national
politics. In the 1640s and 50s this process accelerated dramatically. The Covenanting Wars brought widespread social dislocation and political upheaval in the process of which the
traditional values of Gaeldom gradually became associated with
the royalist cause. Highland support for Charles I was based on
negative rather than positive reasons. Charles was seen as less
likely to meddle in their affairs than the aggressively protestant
Covenanting regime. The identification of the house of Argyll
with the Covenanters automatically inclined many other clans
towards the king. The campaigns of Montrose and Alastair
MacColla between 1644 and 1647 demonstrated the potential of
the Highlanders as a fighting force. MacColla developed the
tactic of the Highland charge, which, in an age of slow-loading
firearms, gave Highlanders an advantage over all but the most
experienced troops. Montrose's initial victory at Tippermuir was

the first time in over 200 years that Highlanders and Lowlanders had clashed in a major battle, inaugurating a century of Highland military involvement in British affairs, which intensified Lowlanders' perceptions of Highlanders as barbarous savages (Stevenson, 1980).

The upheavals of the 1640s and 50s also accelerated another trend among Highland landholders: growing indebtedness. This problem inevitably affected all levels of society as chiefs passed on the burden of their debts to their clansmen through rent increases. Macinnes (1994) cites the example of the MacLeods of Harris and Dunvegan. Sir Rory, who died in 1626, had an annual income of £6,000 and left debts of £12,172. His son, who died in 1649, had an income of £15,000 but left debts of £66,700 and his grandson, who died in 1663, had an income of £18,500 and debts of £129,520. Rents were increasing but debts were outstripping them in a spectacular way. The impact of the Covenanting and Cromwellian Wars greatly increased the scale of indebtedness among Highland landholders. The damage and destruction caused by the campaigns of Montrose drove many landowners on both sides into severe financial difficulties.

Highland military involvement in the Great Rebellion was not confined to the campaigns of Montrose. Highlanders fought in the Engagers' army at Preston and at Worcester. In 1651 the Macleans were almost exterminated fighting Cromwell's forces at Inverkeithing and the Macleods of Skye were nearly destroyed at Worcester. By the 1650s there was a genuine element of royalism in the Highlands, Highlanders finding it easier to give allegiance to a person rather than a policy or institution.

The Cromwellian occupation imposed on the Highlands for the first time effective centralised rule but after the Restoration there was a return to more distant, less effective control by a government preoccupied with quelling opposition to its religious settlement in the Lowlands. Charles II's 'Highland policy' was largely a lazy one of using the existing, imperfect instruments. In the 1660s and 70s the Earl of Argyll was used as a royal lieutenant in the traditional manner. The accumulation of debts from the 1640s and 50s destabilised society, especially in the south west where the Campbells pursued an aggressive policy of expansion, taking over land from the Macleans in lieu of debts in Morvern,

Mull and Tiree. Lawlessness continued but much of it was small-scale banditry rather than major clashes between rival clans. The worst of the trouble was concentrated in specific areas and was often the work of a few groups; the Camerons, the Keppoch and Glencoe MacDonalds and the MacGregors had particularly bad reputations. The upheavals of the mid-seventeenth century had displaced many Highlanders creating bands of 'broken men' and robbers outside the framework of clanship, although their operations sometimes had the tacit approval of local chiefs. As with the Borders a century earlier the increasing concern of the Privy Council over law and order within the Highlands rather than merely when Highlanders impinged on the Lowlands provides a richer written record of crime and violence that may overstate the seriousness of conditions. Feuds were now being pursued by the law rather than by the sword, to the profit of the Edinburgh legal establishment.

By the later seventeenth century the 'Highland problem' was not the same as it had been a century earlier. Clan chiefs could now be brought to heel when the government was really determined. Falling rates of illegitimacy in some areas indicate that church discipline was becoming stronger (Mitchison and Leneman, 1989). The most effective attempt to check violence in the Restoration period was started in 1682 with a Commission of Highland Justiciary, set up without magnates and peers other than those acting as officers of state, and staffed by gentry and chiefs. The Commission could hold courts wherever it thought fit. It could try murderers, thieves and receivers of stolen goods. It decreed that no Highlanders were to sell cattle at a market without a certificate or travel more than seven miles from home carrying arms. In 1683 the Commission met at remote trouble spots like Achallader, Loch Rannoch and Glencoe. It provided an inexpensive and quick means of prosecuting thieves, or their landlords, for compensation.

Most estates in the southern and eastern Highlands, and Lowland ones close to the Highland line, organised their own watch schemes to deter raiding. The government still relied on James VI's policies, with landlords and chiefs being required to give security for their tenants. Commissions of fire and sword were still issued to favoured chiefs and landowners. Various grand designs for re-establishing garrisons at Inverlochy and elsewhere were put forward but always proved too expensive, especially as the small standing army was engaged in operations against Covenanters in the South West.

Debts became an increasing problem in the later seventeenth century. Virtually every Highland landowner seems to have been in debt after 1660. The costs of claiming and settling new areas put financial burdens on the Mackenzies and especially the Campbells. The main way to get out of debt was by further territorial expansion, which, if it did not go successfully, could make matters even worse. Debts encouraged further expansion and the legal actions which this involved; territorial expansion in turn required more cash. An aggressive chief like Campbell of Glenorchy might have two dozen legal actions in progress at once. Maintaining legal agents in Edinburgh and meeting higher taxes imposed further burdens, as did forcing chiefs to pay compensation for losses caused by their clansmen.

It is not too much of an exaggeration to suggest that most of the conflict in the Highlands in the later seventeenth century was the result of debt. The worst of the disorder was caused by the aggression of the Campbells. The Earl of Argyll, with debts of over a million merks used, and misused, his extensive judicial powers to ruin others in order to reduce his own liabilities and avoid destruction. There was some scope for increasing income by raising rents and developing the cattle trade but this could not provide all the cash that was needed. The impact that debt could have on the stability of society is dramatically illustrated by the Campbells of Glenorchy. The family's losses due to Montrose's campaigns were estimated at 1.2 million merks. Their lands suffered further destruction during Glencairn's rising. After 1660 prospects for expanding estates locally were limited. The family tried to emulate the Campbells of Cawdor, a cadet branch of the Campbells with a base in the North East, who had successfully built up a scattered empire by acquiring Islay. Glenorchy turned his attention to Caithness, buying up the Earl of Caithness' debts and eventually acquiring his estates through the process of appraisal. After the Earl died in 1676 Glenorchy also took over the Caithness title by bribing the Duchess of Lauderdale to influence her husband, Charles II's

Scottish secretary, to confirm him. The Duchess exacted a high price and Glenorchy had to borrow yet more money to pay her. The heir of the former earl was his cousin, George Sinclair of Keiss. In 1677 he began a counter attack to regain by force the lands that he considered to be rightfully his. The result was a minor civil war in the far north culminating in a pitched battle in 1680 in which Glenorchy (now Earl of Caithness) defeated Sinclair, killing over 100 of his followers.

Economic developments in the Highlands in the later seventeenth and early eighteenth centuries involved attempts by landowners to diversify their activities and expand their incomes. An uncertain influence on economic conditions was the degree of population pressure. There are indirect indications of a build-up of population from the later sixteenth century, shown by an expansion of cultivation and a change from the use of ploughs to more laborious but more productive hand tillage with spade and cas chrom (foot plough) (Dodgshon, 1993). The short-term demographic impact of the mid-seventeenth-century upheavals and the famines of the later 1690s is unclear but on a timescale of decades the more generally peaceful conditions of the later seventeenth and early eighteenth centuries are likely to have encouraged a rise of population. The growth of the cattle trade during this period has been seen as a positive reaction to closer links with the Lowlands and with England. However, viewed more pessimistically, it may also have been a symptom of an economy under pressure, needing more money to pay for increasing imports of meal from the Lowlands in order to survive. Profits from the cattle trade were becoming vital to the Highland economy. Other activities were geared to increasing the cash incomes of chiefs. In 1678 Cameron of Locheil commissioned a blast furnace near his home at Achnacarry, the first to be initiated by a Highland landowner.

The increasing integration of the Highlands and Lowlands in the later seventeenth century is also seen in the growing numbers of Highlanders in the Lowlands. They were becoming familiar as drovers and seasonal harvest workers. By the end of the seventeenth century towns like Stirling, Perth and Glasgow had substantial populations of Highlanders. Edinburgh's first Gaelic chapel was established in 1708.

In seeking greater contact with the Lowlands ordinary High-landers were merely following the example of their chiefs. The lives of many Highland landowners were becoming increasingly cosmopolitan and expensive in the later seventeenth century. Sir George Mackenzie of Tarbat, later first Earl of Cromartie, is a striking instance. He was the grandson of the violent Sir Rorie who carved out with his sword a little empire in Ross-shire early in the seventeenth century. Educated at the universities of St Andrews and Aberdeen, trained in law, he became a major political figure in Restoration Scotland, remarkable for his survival skills, serving no less than six monarchs. Urbane and civilised, he was a founder member of the Royal Society, to which he contributed papers. Unlike his father and grandfather he was an absentee landlord for much of the time, living in Edinburgh, managing his estates through chamberlains and having little direct contact with his tenants. His expensive lifestyle culminated in the purchase of a small estate near Edinburgh and the construction of a mansion, Royston House. His attitude to his estates was clearly that they were a source of money, one which became increasingly inade-quate in the face of rising expenditure in Edinburgh and London. He was active in the grain trade between Easter Ross and Edin-burgh but his predatory attitude towards his lands is emphasised by his depletion of the woods of Coigach in the far north west of Ross-shire. In 1712, in his early 80s, he retired to his northern estates. His aim, however, was to live frugally for a few years in order to accumulate enough cash for a final spree in London! By the time of his death the estates were in severe financial difficul-ties. His example is almost the antithesis of the popular notion of a traditional Highland landlord and demonstrates how readily even the greatest of such men could bring financial disaster on their estates through trying to match the lifestyles of English magnates (Richards and Clough, 1989).

Social and Economic Change in the Early Eighteenth Century

During the first half of the eighteenth century the traditional role of the tacksmen came increasingly under threat. They began to be seen by some Highland proprietors as obstacles to improvement who rack-rented and oppressed the small tenants. Because they creamed off a higher surplus from the tenantry than they paid to their chiefs the removal of tacksmen on an estate could give a proprietor additional income without necessarily raising the tenants' rents. By the end of the seventeenth century tenurial arrangements characterised by direct proprietor–tenant relationships without intermediate tacksmen had started to appear. The removal of the tacksmen class occurred most dramatically on the Argyll estates during the first half of the eighteenth century (Cregeen, 1969). The initiative taken by the Dukes of Argyll in estate reorganisation and improvement has sometimes been seen as an example of forward-looking, progressive management. Lindsay and Cosh (1972) have suggested that the second Duke was only interested in squeezing more money out of his estates to support an increasingly ostentatious lifestyle.

He began removing tacksmen in Kintyre from about 1710. The rents that the tacksmen were paying had already been rising steadily. These rises were inevitably passed on to the tenants who began to identify the tacksmen with the estate administration rather than with the interests of the ordinary people. In 1737 there was a more widespread reorganisation of tenures on Campbell lands in Mull, Morvern and Tiree. The tacksmen system was abolished and written leases were offered to the former tenants, mostly at higher rents. A quarter of the leases, but three quarters of the land, went to the former tacksmen who, with their accumulated capital, were able to bid for groups of farms. They retained their social dominance, though it was now based on economic rather than traditional sources of power. By removing the key group that had linked the house of Argyll with the ordinary Campbell clansman these reforms virtually dismantled the clan system. Competitive bidding pushed rents up substantially. Argyll's own estate administrators, more closely in touch with economic reality in the West Highlands than their master, protested. In their view moderate rents fully paid were preferable to high rents and high arrears.

The reforms were pushed through at a time when cattle prices were sluggish. Within a year or two rent arrears began to rise alarmingly. Bad weather in the early 1740s caused heavy losses of livestock and many bankrupt tenants were forced to abandon their holdings. When the third Duke succeeded in 1743 he showed a greater appreciation of the nature of the crisis by reducing some rents. The removal of the tacksmen as figures of authority helps to explain the failure of the Campbells to mobilise against the Jacobites in 1745; the structure of the clan had been destroyed by commercialisation. It is not clear how far the removal of tacksmen had gone elsewhere in the Highlands by the 1750s but although they may have led the field, it is unlikely that the Argyll estates were unique.

There was a spurt of English investment in the Highlands after the failure of the 1715 rebellion. Mining and timber extraction were two main areas of development. Both activities were embraced by the York Buildings Company, formed to supply London with water but relaunched by a group of speculators with the aim of acquiring forfeited Jacobite estates (Cummings, 1994). Their over-optimistic and mismanaged approach was to pour cash into ventures using inappropriately advanced technology in unsuitable locations and circumstances. Their timber and iron smelting venture in Abernethy Forest and their lead mining activities at Strontian produced results but not on a par with the scale of investment. More modest schemes might have been more successful; their ideas outstripped commercial reality.

The Highlands remained a focus of Jacobite activity throughout the first half of the eighteenth century partly because the nature of clan society made this the only part of Britain in which a force of trained fighting men could be quickly mobilised. The danger that this presented to the government was appreciated after 1715; radical schemes to dismantle Highland society were proposed in 1716 and 1724 but were not implemented. In the years after the 1715 rebellion the Highlands were more stable than they had been for a long time; the region's problem was not endemic violence but poverty and lack of economic development, along with increasing population pressure.

The 1745 rebellion shook the government so severely that in the aftermath of Culloden there were no half-measures. Government involvement in the region initially took the form of restoring and increasing garrisons, and mounting punitive expeditions against the lands of Jacobite clans. The abolition of wardholding and heritable jurisdictions in 1747 formed part of a sustained attack on the structure of clanship, which aimed to destroy the political separateness of the Highlands. A disarming act, more rigorously enforced than earlier ones, was imposed and wearing Highland dress was forbidden. Despite these measures it was economic rather than political change that undermined traditional Highland society. Once central authority was firmly in control of the region, government involvement began to take on social and economic as well as military dimensions. The impact of this, however, has often been exaggerated. Social and economic conditions in the Highlands had been changing gradually for a century and a half or more. Much of the change that occurred after 1745 would have happened anyway even if the rebellion had not taken place. Government policy aimed at social and economic development in order to integrate the Highlands more closely with the rest of Britain. The philosophy of 'improvement' was extended from the Lowlands. The untapped productive forces of the Highlands, it was thought, could be usefully employed in manufacturing or in military service.

A good deal of attention has been focused on the activities and supposed achievements of various official bodies in the Highlands after the 1745 rebellion. The example of the Annexed Forfeited Estates demonstrates the need to examine critically the work of such organisations (Smith, 1982). Forty-one forfeited Scottish estates were taken over by the Barons of Exchequer. Most were auctioned off but 13 were annexed to the crown in 1752. Three years later a body of commissioners – crown officials, nobles, lairds and lawyers – was appointed to oversee the management of the estates, which were spread over 30 parishes from near Stirling to Coigach in the far north. The idea behind the management of the forfeited estates was that the rents paid by tenants could be ploughed back into agricultural improvement and other development. Unfortunately, the over-bureaucratic administration absorbed much of the surplus while obstruction by tenants slowed the pace of those improvements which were tried. Some useful work was done in financing road and bridge building schemes but this was done in an unco-ordinated, piecemeal fashion. Much of the well-intentioned paternalism of the Commissioners had little effect. They were the first in a series of bodies aimed at promoting regional development in the Highlands that came to grief through insufficient funds, unsuitable policies and the intractable nature of both the land and its inhabitants.

* * *

Attempts to transform the Highlands from outside were rarely as successful as those generated internally. Less studied, but probably of much greater significance, were the slow but widespread changes that were taking place on many other Highland estates as landowners finally abandoned all but a few residual elements of clanship and began to exploit their estates for pure commercial gain. Chief–clansman relations changed gradually to landlord–tenant ones as chiefs came to view their lands in terms of their economic resources rather than the number of fighting men they could maintain. As the region came increasingly under centralised control its inhabitants, for a while, may have become more prosperous. An end to unrest and political instability, agricultural improvement, the spread of the potato, the expansion of the cattle trade, spinning linen yarn, fishing, mining and forestry all generated additional income, as did seasonal employment in the Lowland harvest. Much of the income, however, went to the landowners rather than their tenants, and the inevitable effect of this modest phase of prosperity and a broadening in the means of subsistence as the Highlands were opened to the impact of commercial influences was an acceleration of population growth, which was to wipe out any gains in standards of living and lead to drastic new reassessments of the balance between manpower and economic development in the region.

6

TOWN AND COUNTRY

In 1500 Scotland was a country without large towns and cities, comparable in many respects to Scandinavia and other outlying regions of Europe and contrasting sharply with countries like France, Italy and Spain, which had many cities with populations of over 10,000. This situation barely altered for much of the sixteenth century. By the early seventeenth century, however, Scotland's urban population was starting to grow. By the 1750s over 9 per cent of the population lived in towns with over 10,000 inhabitants and 16 per cent in towns with over 2,000. Scotland was fast becoming one of the most urbanised societies in Europe.

Patterns of Urbanisation

In the early sixteenth century Scottish towns were at the end of a prolonged period of stagnation and decay caused by a slump in overseas trade. Between then and the early eighteenth century the proportion of Scotland's population living in towns with over 10,000 inhabitants increased from around 1.6 per cent to 5.3 per cent, compared with 3.1 per cent to 13.3 per cent for England (Whyte, 1989). Scotland had one of the highest growth rates of urban population in Europe. During the later sixteenth and early seventeenth centuries most towns appear to have increased in size but in the majority of cases the available data are insufficient for even a guess at urban populations. While this was a period of demographic growth generally some towns seem to have grown faster than the overall rate of population increase. Although the impact of this phase of growth on urban societies and economies has yet to be fully evaluated, it is clear that it put severe strains on the administrative and social frameworks of the medieval burgh (Lynch, 1987).

The 1630s represented a peak of growth and prosperity before the disruption, damage and impoverishment caused by the Covenanting Wars, a severe outbreak of bubonic plague in the mid-1640s and the Cromwellian occupation. Between 1660 and 1700 the overall urban population grew modestly, if at all, significant growth being confined to Edinburgh, Glasgow and a limited number of smaller centres, while many medium-sized and small towns stagnated or even lost population (Lynch, 1991). English urban growth has been seen as distinctive in a European context where the percentage of the population in towns with over 5,000 inhabitants did not rise markedly between 1500 and 1800 but the rate of urban growth in Scotland was equally impressive (de Vries, 1985). If England diverged from the pattern of European urbanization at some time during the early-modern period, Scotland had already started to do so by the first half of the eighteenth century.

In the early sixteenth century the Scottish urban system was still only partially integrated. The burghs developed a national political lobby before they formed an integrated urban network. Groups of burghs, like those of the North East or around the Firth of Tay, were only loosely tied into a national economic framework. In the sixteenth century the urban hierarchy was dominated by Edinburgh, Aberdeen, Dundee and Perth, joined in the seventeenth century by Glasgow. In 1535 the 'big four' paid 52 per cent of burgh taxation, in 1613 54 per cent. By 1697, however, the pattern had changed, with 55 per cent being paid by Edinburgh and Glasgow, the former accounting for 40 per cent. The seventeenth century saw the slippage of Aberdeen, Dundee and Perth. In 1705 they paid only half the share of burgh taxation that they had paid in 1535.

Despite a substantial increase in the proportion of the population living in towns during this period, Scotland was still lightly urbanised in the first half of the eighteenth century compared with England. The Highlands barely contained any centres that could be described as urban. Much of the Lowlands, outside the central belt, were served only by small settlements, barely urban, with populations of a few hundred, and the occasional larger town with perhaps 2,000 inhabitants. By contrast the area around the Firth of Forth had become a highly urbanised region, with around 40 per cent of the population living in towns by the 1690s, a figure comparable with parts of the Netherlands (Lynch, 1991). The implications of this concentration of urban population for the Scottish economy have not been fully considered but there was undoubted spin-off into agriculture and industries like coal mining and salt manufacture.

The Scottish urban hierarchy was not dominated by a single over-large primate city like England or Ireland. Edinburgh only held $c.4.7$ per cent of Scotland's population in the 1690s compared with London's $c.10$ per cent of England's population. In the seventeenth century Edinburgh was little more than twice the size of the second city, Glasgow. The combined populations of Glasgow, Aberdeen, Dundee and Perth equalled or exceeded that of the capital. This suggests that in Scotland the role of the major regional centres was greater than south of the Border, reflecting the strong element of localism within Scottish society.

Below the major regional centres there was a lack of medium-sized towns and a long tail of very small centres. The minimum population size defining a town in Scotland was possibly around 500 in 1700 compared with $c.1,000$ for England. The urban hierarchy in 1639 consisted of about 60 towns, 36 under $c.2,500$, 10 over 5,000 but only 9 in the 2,500–5,000 range. The pattern for the later seventeenth century was similar. In 1639 towns with between 2,000 and 10,000 inhabitants had almost as many inhabitants as those with over 10,000. In the 1690s hearth and poll tax data suggest that towns with between 1,000 and 5,000 inhabitants held $c.6.6$ per cent of the population against $c.7.2$ per cent for ones with over 10,000. These small towns would have been many rural dwellers' normal experience of urban life, in contrast to Ireland where small towns were few and far between (Whyte, 1989).

As trade revived in the sixteenth century Edinburgh acquired an increasing share of many sectors of Scottish trade, especially wool and leather, without a corresponding increase in population. As early as 1480 Edinburgh accounted for 54 per cent of Scotland's export revenues. By 1578 this had risen to 75 per cent (Lynch, 1987). By the later sixteenth century the dominance of

Edinburgh over Scottish trade was even greater than that of London over English commerce. Edinburgh had less of a grip on exports of fish, coal and salt, which explains the prominence of many small ports around the Forth until markets for these commodities began to decline in the late seventeenth century. Edinburgh's increasing monopoly of foreign trade in the sixteenth century led to the other large regional centres focusing more on internal trade, acting as feeders to Edinburgh. They appear to have done this, however, at the expense of middle-rank towns.

The Institutional Context

An appreciation of the institutional context of Scottish burghs is essential for understanding the urban system. By the sixteenth century two groups of burghs had emerged: royal burghs and burghs of barony. In the first half of the sixteenth century the royal burghs were consolidating a system of monopolies that was strong by European standards. They were developing into a homogeneous group with an ability to define and pursue common aims, which allowed them to maintain their monopolies into the later seventeenth century. Their privileges were granted by the crown in return for a major contribution to national taxation. Their solidarity was reinforced by the development of the Convention of Royal Burghs, an independent assembly free from direct control, to which each royal burgh sent representatives. The Convention was unique in Europe, created by the burghs themselves rather than the crown, reflecting the *laissez-faire* approach of the Scottish monarchy. The Convention apportioned the burghs' contributions to royal taxation, regulated their affairs, promoted their interests and defended their rights.

The merchants of each royal burgh had the sole right to carry on overseas trade within a specified hinterland or 'liberty', which might embrace an entire sheriffdom. There is no parallel in Western Europe for the size of the liberties of some Scottish royal burghs nor the completeness with which the country was carved up. In the sixteenth and seventeenth centuries the creation of new royal burghs was resisted by existing ones because the liberties of the new foundations had to be carved out of those of the old. Internal trade within the liberty of a royal burgh was also, supposedly, confined to the burgh's market place, although this rule was often ignored. From the fifteenth century burghs of barony began to be founded. They were authorised by the crown but held from lay and ecclesiastical landowners. They were forbidden to engage in foreign trade and their merchants could only buy and sell within the confines of the burgh, rather than in the surrounding countryside, which fell within a royal burgh liberty. Some 250 baronial burghs were founded between 1500 and the Union of 1707. By the late sixteenth and early seventeenth centuries many of them were encroaching on the privileges of the royal burghs. The full privileges of the royal burghs were confirmed in 1633 but the very fact that such a confirmation was considered necessary suggests that their position was under attack.

After the Restoration the tide of opinion began to turn against the royal burghs, whose monopolies were increasingly seen as restrictive. A number of baronial burghs developed to challenge long-established royal burghs. A good example is Old Aberdeen, lying to the north of the royal burgh of Aberdeen. After the Restoration the authorities of Old Aberdeen made vigorous efforts to revive the town's traditional fairs with such success that in the later seventeenth century Old Aberdeen doubled in size from c.900 to c.1,800 inhabitants while the population of Aberdeen declined (Tyson, 1991). Trade increased and the town held far greater concentrations of merchants and craftsmen in the 1690s than in the 1630s. An act of 1672 gave baronial burghs most of the rights to foreign trade possessed by royal burghs. The growth in the number of baronial burghs and their increased privileges after 1672 has been seen as marking a shift in the control of the economy from the towns to rural landowners. This in turn had an impact on urban institutions. The royal burghs won back some concessions in 1691 but the old system of monopolies had been effectively dismantled. The Convention of Royal Burghs turned its attention in the late seventeenth and early eighteenth centuries to trying to transfer a proportion of the royal burghs' tax burden on to the baronial burghs whose trade, in some cases, was beginning to rival and even surpass their own.

In the fifteenth and sixteenth centuries many burghs, even large ones, came under the influence of local nobles and gentry who offered protection at the price of interference in their affairs. Aberdeen formalised this process in 1463 by entering into a bond of manrent with the Earl of Huntly. With royal authority distant and the power of the Gordons so strong in the North East this was a sensible arrangement. The Gordons used it to install one of their client families, the Menzies of Pitfodels, as virtual hereditary provosts of Aberdeen until the end of the sixteenth century. Members of the Menzies family held the provostship for 68 of the first 80 years of the sixteenth century.

The fragmented pattern of landownership around Edinburgh reduced the problem of local magnate dominance but the city's status led to the danger of noble provosts being installed by the crown or by court factions during minorities. Nevertheless, in larger towns like Aberdeen the influence of noble patrons was not absolute and could be disputed by the burgesses while other landed families might try to plant their clients on the council. This could lead to problems when a town formed an arena for feuding landed families as in the case of Stirling in the 1550s and 1560s, whose inhabitants were caught up in a struggle between the Erskines and the Livingstons. The winners, the Erskines, packed the council with client lairds. In smaller burghs the relationship with landed patrons was closer, more direct and often more beneficial. Peebles had a long-standing relationship with the Hays of Yester, a middle-rank noble family that held the office of provost throughout the second half of the sixteenth century. The Hays were also hereditary sheriffs with their seat at Neidpath Castle just outside the town. The family interceded on behalf of the town at the central law courts and the royal court in Edinburgh, notably in a series of disputes concerning encroachment on burgh lands by local lairds (Lynch, 1987).

There was a lessening of interest by landowners in burgh government in the second half of James VI's reign; lairds and nobles retired to their estates and left the merchants, craftsmen and sometimes lawyers to run the towns. The change was signalled in Aberdeen by the ousting of the Menzies dynasty in the 1590s, marking a move towards closer links between burghs and central government.

As royal power in the localities grew during the sixteenth century towns were increasingly drawn into national affairs. A result of a series of political crises beginning with the Reformation in 1560 encouraged unprecented interference in burgh affairs by central government on one hand and a much more co-ordinated urban voice in national politics on the other. Royal or court interference in burgh affairs involved the installation of royal nominees as provosts in Edinburgh, Perth and other key towns, and sometimes the purging of entire councils. The worst encroachments on burgh independence came not under strong kings but during royal minorities. Another aspect of royal interest in the burghs was a rapidly increasing burden of taxation. By the later sixteenth century, partly as a result of these new pressures, royal burghs, under the Convention, had become a highly organised and coherent political lobby. The mid-1580s marked the peak of royal interference in burgh affairs until the reign of James VII. An act of 1609 ended an age of noble provosts as royal nominees, but did not end noble influence in the burghs. At Peebles the Hays stepped down as provosts but continued to serve as 'ordinary' councillors (Lynch, 1987).

In late-medieval times the inhabitants of the towns, like Scottish society as a whole, had been relatively lightly taxed. Taxation of the burghs began to rise from the 1530s but increased dramatically in the reign of James VI. Not only were taxes imposed with increasing frequency but there was also a considerable increase in the number of taxpayers, including groups like sons of merchants, lawyers and occasional residents such as lairds and merchants from other burghs. A broader range of activities was also assessed. Greater concern over taxation and threats to their privileges is shown by the Convention's appointment of an agent to lobby Parliament and the Privy Council from the 1590s and the court in London from 1613. In 1597 the wholesale revision of customs duties, additional levies on wine and a 5 per cent tax on imports doubled crown revenue, mostly at the expense of the urban sector. A tax on annual rents, or interest on loans, in 1621 was even more controversial, coming at the peak of urban prosperity. Taxation increased again under Charles I. In the first 20 months of his reign Edinburgh paid more tax than in the last 25 years of James VI's reign. Taxation rose still further under the Covenanting regime after 1638 with desperate attempts to raise money by 'voluntary' loans and the surrender of gold and silverwork as well as conventional taxes, plus local military exactions and quartering (Stevenson, 1987). Between March and June 1639 occupation of Aberdeen by royalist and Covenanting armies cost the town £19,313 Scots compared with £1,333 for a normal year's taxation. By the mid-seventeenth century urban populations had become the most highly taxed sector of Scottish society.

Urbanization and Agricultural Change

The scale of urban growth in early-modern Scotland has many implications. The increasing urban population required feeding. That it *was* fed and that a substantial volume of grain was exported during the first two decades of the seventeenth century, and in most years during the later seventeenth and early eighteenth centuries, suggests that productivity per head in Scottish agriculture may have been rising, albeit modestly, whether through the development of improved techniques or better organisation. Certainly urban growth on this scale elsewhere has been linked to rises in productivity per head in agriculture. In Scotland the proportion of the population outside towns with more than 2,000 inhabitants fell from *c.*98 per cent in 1560 to *c.*88 per cent by 1700 while food supply improved markedly. The supply of food to the growing towns must also have had an impact on transport and internal trading. To what extent increasing demand for food from urban populations generated greater prosperity in the countryside, and whether any of this penetrated below the level of the landowners, has yet to be determined.

Early-modern Scottish towns, including Edinburgh, were small in area and often not very densely built up. Gordon of Rothiemay, writing in 1660, described Aberdeen, the third most important town: 'mony houses have ther gardings and orcheyards adjoyning. Every garding hes its posterne and thes are planted with all sorts of trees... so that the quhole toune... looks as if it stood in a garding or little wood'. Agriculture was an important full- and part-time employer in smaller towns and was also significant in the larger ones. In Dumfries, twelfth in the tax roll of royal burghs in 1649, 36 of 66 merchants between 1600 and 1665 showed evidence of direct involvement in agriculture. Some owned cows and sheep within the town's limits or nearby for purely domestic supplies (Coutts, 1987). Some had a couple of acres of arable land. Others were involved in farming on a larger, more commercial, scale. Many merchants and tradesmen, even in quite large towns, possessed shares in the arable lands and common grazings of their burghs. Others, especially in the larger centres, leased land beyond the town limits. Town dwellers' livestock were grazed on the burghs' common pastures, which could be extensive. In smaller towns, where little infilling of burgage plots had occurred, a good deal of produce came from gardens and orchards within the burgh limits. Even larger towns like Aberdeen drew a substantial proportion of their grain from lands belonging to the burgh. Acts of burgh courts in towns like Lanark and Peebles show that many hens, pigs and cattle were kept within the urban area (Whyte, 1979). Even late seventeenth-century Edinburgh had cow feeders and gardeners in the less densely built-up Canongate while a considerable proportion of the population obtained temporary employment in the surrounding countryside at harvest time. In smaller centres the full-time agricultural element rose dramatically, accounting for up to 40 per cent of the recorded male population (Whyte, 1987).

Although the impact of towns on agriculture within their hinterlands has yet to be studied systematically, it is clear that it was considerable. In their immediate environs were zones of intensive cultivation. Rotations concentrating on bere for brewing, and probably using urban refuse as a manure, are recorded from around Aberdeen. In the 1630s landowners outside Edinburgh carried urban refuse up to four miles from the city. Rents of tenements close to towns were higher per unit area than those further away, implying more intensive cultivation and greater yields. More generally the impact of Edinburgh on agriculture in the Lothians can be seen in the relatively intensive farming systems and more commercialised farm structures that developed in this region during the seventeenth century. In the 1610s and 20s agriculture in the Lothians was transformed by the widespread adoption of liming. This allowed an expansion of the arable area, the conversion of outfield to infield, more intensive cropping of outfields, higher yields and substantial increases in rents. Liming may also have encouraged the use of legumes which in turn promoted soil fertility (Whyte, 1979, 'Agriculture and Society'). The impact on agriculture in areas with easy access to the Edinburgh market can be seen on the Dundas estates near South Queensferry, where liming began in 1624 and an intensive farming system geared to grain production had developed by the 1630s (Whyte, 1979, 'Agriculture and Society'). The extent to which such developments were related to the penetration of Edinburgh merchant capital has yet to be investigated but it cannot be a coincidence that they were contemporary with a phase of rapid growth in both population and trade.

By the later seventeenth century the Lothians were also unusual in terms of their farm and holding structures. As was noted in Chapter 2 the poll tax records of 1694 show that in this area multiple tenancy was relatively rare and large, single-tenant farms worked mainly by hired servants were common, suggesting that tenants in the Lothians were already well on the way to becoming commercialised and involved in the market (Devine, 1994). As tenant numbers fell and holding size rose more and more farmers must have found themselves with marketable surpluses. Tenant reduction and increase in average holding size gave farmers greater capacity to respond to market opportunities. In the late seventeenth and early eighteenth centuries there was also an important sectoral shift around Edinburgh and Glasgow towards livestock production, with arable land being laid down to grass, probably associated with rising living standards for some sectors of the urban population and a move towards diets with a greater component of meat and dairy products (Dodgshon, 1981).

Towns affected the countryside in other ways. Towns were important providers of credit for rural society. Early seventeenth-century Aberdeen was a net provider of credit for its rural hinterland (Macniven, 1977). Merchants in the larger towns also invested in rural property, not usually the purchase of estates to gain social prestige but strictly for business purposes. Although individual merchants can be traced buying estates from the fourteenth century, Scottish merchants as a group were active in purchasing land mainly on a small-scale, short-term basis. A successful early sixteenth-century Aberdeen merchant like Sir John Rutherford preferred to invest in urban rather than rural property, as did wealthier craftsmen (Booton, 1982). Of the 11 élite merchant families in Aberdeen at this time only two had built up substantial estates although by the early seventeenth century landholding was rather more widespread among the élite merchants.

In early seventeenth-century Edinburgh it was the lawyers who led the move into rural property and were far more likely to ape the gentry than merchants. The activities of Edinburgh's merchant élite relating to land expanded rapidly from the 1590s. It was the credit system rather than social ambitions which brought Edinburgh merchants and rural estates together at this time, an arrangement that did not survive the Wars of the Covenant. Edinburgh merchants lent money on wadset to rural landowners, which gave them control of the land and its products in lieu of rent. Although their involvement in land was widespread, there was a concentration on east-coast arable areas, suggesting links with the grain trade, much of which was in their hands. Although they were not directly involved in cultivation, it is likely that their capital lay behind the changes in agricultural systems in the Lothians in the early seventeenth century noted above (Brown, 1985).

In the first four decades of the seventeenth century more and more of Scotland's trade came into the hands of a small, increasingly prosperous élite of Edinburgh merchants. The scale and range of their activities has only recently been appreciated. As their wealth increased they diversified into new activities outside the city, investing in lead and coal mining, salt production, herring curing and cloth making. The boom in salt production in Fife in the first three decades of the century was probably due directly to Edinburgh merchant capital. Although Edinburgh's élite were experiencing difficulties in the early 1630s, the bubble burst spectacularly with the outbreak of the Covenanting Wars in 1638. War, plague, unpaid loans, high taxes and forced requisitions ruined the most prominent members of this group (Stevenson, 1987). Edinburgh's trade collapsed and a different economy emerged in the later seventeenth century, with Edinburgh less dominant than previously.

After the Restoration merchants from Edinburgh and other large towns had only a limited impact on the land market until the mid-eighteenth century. In the charters of the Great Seal for the early decades of the seventeenth century 60 per cent of transactions involved merchants, the bulk of them from Edinburgh. Between 1660 and 1668 under 6 per cent of all transactions involved merchants, 61 per cent from Edinburgh, 20 per cent from Glasgow and Aberdeen. As in the early part of the century they rarely purchased estates. Land came into their hands mainly through apprisings due to debts, an accidental result of the commercial regime rather than a means of withdrawing from trade. Of the 239 merchants listed in the Aberdeen poll tax returns for 1695 only seven owned estates. The Skenes of Rubislaw in Aberdeen and the Campbells of Shawfield in Glasgow are rare examples of merchant families who severed their links with trade after acquiring estates.

Little information has so far been uncovered about the pattern of the grain trade in the late sixteenth and early seventeenth centuries during the most rapid phase of urban growth, although at this time Edinburgh was drawing grain supplies from as far away as the Moray Firth. Early seventeenth-century Aberdeen received some of its grain from its local hinterland but also drew on areas further north including Buchan, the Black Isle and Ross, a good deal of it for re-export. On the east coast tenants paid their rents mainly in grain and were frequently required to deliver it to the nearest coastal royal burgh or sometimes to landowners' own harbours for shipment (Whyte, 1979, 'Agriculture and Society').

From the 1660s food supply improved markedly, a crucial regulator of everything from demand for manufactured goods to Scotland's balance of payments. The problems of farmers and landlords became those of food surplus rather than grain shortage. By the end of the seventeenth century the hinterland supplying grain to Edinburgh for direct consumption and export extended from Orkney to Berwickshire and periodically to north eastern England. Edinburgh brewers were major customers for barley from as far away as Easter Ross and Orkney. At a regional scale there were movements of grain from the Moray Firth to Aberdeen and Dundee, and from Caithness to Inverness (Whyte,

1979, 'Agriculture and Society'). Most of Glasgow's supplies came from the west-central Lowlands but by the end of the century the town appears to have outstripped the capacity of this area to supply it and was shipping grain from east coast estates. By the early eighteenth century Glasgow was also importing significant quantities of grain from Ireland. Some landowners invested substantially in infrastructure to cash in on the grain trade, such as the Earl of Cromartie who financed the construction of a harbour and granaries at Portmahomack in 1689. In most cases the grain was sold by landowners to merchants who arranged for the shipping but on occasion landowners cut out the middlemen, taking the more risky option of hiring granaries in Edinburgh or Leith and doing the marketing themselves.

The economic role of the rash of new market centres that spread across Scotland in the sixteenth and seventeenth centuries is not clear. Seigneurial foundations had been slow to develop in Scotland compared with England. In addition to the 250 baronial burghs founded between 1500 and the early eighteenth century, between 1660 and 1707 nearly 150 non-burghal markets and fairs were licensed and there is also evidence of the operation of unlicensed trading centres (Whyte, 1979, 'Periodic Markets'). Some baronial burghs, like the coal and salt towns around the Firth of Forth, had an industrial base but most were established with the aim of generating or capturing trade. There are parallels with Ireland, where hundreds of new market centres were authorised in the seventeenth century. It is possible that many of the Scottish centres had a similar function of channelling agricultural produce and rural manufactures such as cloth towards the larger towns.

Only a small proportion of these centres developed into towns and few of those which did grew sufficiently to move out of the lowest levels of the urban hierarchy. Most landowners who were granted burgh charters were probably only seeking to attach market and fair rights to existing rural settlements without any intention of promoting further development. Fairs at locations of this type could develop into gatherings of regional significance. Much of Aberdeen's trade passed through the fairs of Culsalmond, Old Rayne and Kincardine. Some proprietors did lay out planned settlements with burgages and create institutions with a degree of self-government, although most of the costs of development were often passed on to the inhabitants. Instances of large-scale capital investment by landowners are less common but the examples of the Earl of Winton at Port Seton, the Earl of Wemyss at Methil, the Duke of Hamilton at Bo'ness and Sir Robert Cunningham at Saltcoats should be noted. The Erskines of Mar turned Alloa from a squalid collier village into a thriving town with an integrated programme of development (Smout, 1963).

We know little about the function of these smaller centres, the amount of trade they handled, the revenues they generated and the attitudes of the landowners who promoted them. The factors that encouraged some baronial burghs to achieve urban status appear to have included a reasonable distance from competing royal burghs, a degree of landlord involvement, a range of functions providing a basis for development and the ability to generate trade at more than a local level. Langholm in Dumfries-shire, established in 1671, and Thurso in Caithness, which received its charter in 1633, are good examples of settlements that managed the transition from rural market centre to small town.

It is difficult to be sure to what extent the spread of such new centres reflected an expansion or merely a redistribution of trade. Some, like Crieff, which developed as a centre for the Highland cattle trade, were associated with new trends in the economy. In other cases new centres seem to have been designed by their founders to capture trade from nearby royal burghs. Sir George Mackenzie, writing in 1669, considered that the creation of so many new market centres was detrimental by spreading the existing volume of trade through too many small outlets. The traditional view has been that the royal burghs were more concerned with privilege than progress, that the roots of economic advance in the later seventeenth century lay in the countryside, with baronial burghs being developed by landowners outside the control of reactionary urban oligarchies. This picture has probably been overdrawn. In a report to the Convention of Royal Burghs in 1692 many middle-rank and smaller royal burghs complained bitterly about the loss of trade to the new upstarts (Whyte, 1979, 'Periodic Markets'). Perth listed 24 such centres that were in competition with the town. However, merchants of larger royal burghs exploited the smaller centres for their own benefit circumventing traditional monopolies by entering into partnerships with traders in baronial burghs. In 1692 Dundee admitted trading links with at least 15 unfree towns and villages. Glasgow's commercial position was vitally dependent on satellites like Greenock, Paisley and Port Glasgow. Edinburgh's satellite baronial burghs, closely tied to the city's economy, included Bo'ness, Dalkeith, Musselburgh and Prestonpans (Whyte, 1987). The current view is that in the later seventeenth century rigidities in the domestic economy began to relax and commodity exchange increased, with a vigorous coastal trade in grain, salt and coal.

Migration, Mobility and Vagrancy

For the larger towns to grow as they did, especially in the late sixteenth and early seventeenth centuries, there must have been a steady influx of migrants from the countryside, especially young, single people like apprentices and servants. Given the concentration of urban population around the Firth of Forth by the end of the seventeenth century there must have been a substantial net movement of population into this region from other parts of Scotland. By analogy with London, late seventeenth-century Edinburgh may have required a minimum of 300 and perhaps around 400 migrants a year to make up for mortality and allow for growth. Glasgow, Dundee and Aberdeen may have required another 350–500. This represents a movement into the largest towns of up to 900 people a year, a significant amount when it is considered that emigration during the seventeenth century was only about twice this level. These figures only represent net migration. Assuming a substantial counterflow from town to country the gross total of new arrivals each year would have been considerably larger.

How much of the urban in-migration in the late sixteenth and early seventeenth centuries was due to push factors, as has been suggested for sixteenth-century England? There is little direct evidence but rapid price inflation, periodic dearth and the knock-on effects of the shake-up in landownership caused by the feuing of church and crown lands is likely to have encouraged movement to the towns. There was a growing problem of poverty in late sixteenth-century Scotland and it was seen by Parliament as essentially an urban phenomenon.

Lowland Scotland shared with England a pattern of high levels of population mobility in the countryside, although generally over fairly limited distances (Houston, 1985). As in England, rural–urban migration was an important element in population mobility. Although comparative rates of urban and rural mortality for this period are not known, it is likely that Scotland's larger towns, like their counterparts elsewhere in Europe, had higher child and adult mortality levels than the countryside. This is hinted at indirectly in the high rates of turnover of urban property. Edinburgh in particular had an awkward, tightly packed site, which posed particular problems for water supply and waste disposal. In Edinburgh and its immediate environs the outbreak of plague in 1644–45 is estimated to have killed up to 12,000 people, as much as a third of the population.

Famine too affected urban populations down to the end of the seventeenth century. In Aberdeen the famines of the later 1690s resulted in a drop of population of over 20 per cent between 1695 and 1700 (Tyson, 1986). Such disasters were commonly followed by waves of migrants seeking opportunities. Apprenticeship migration to Edinburgh in the wake of the plague outbreak of 1644 was almost three times the level of previous years (Lovett *et al.*, 1985). In Aberdeen the plague outbreak of 1647–48 killed around 1,700 and was followed by the immigration of hundreds of people who, along with the arrival of the 1,000 strong Cromwellian garrison in 1650, unbalanced the age structure of the city's population (Desbrisay, 1986).

Information on urban in-migration is heavily slanted towards a few relatively well-recorded groups. Patterns of apprenticeship migration to the main Scottish towns are fairly clear. Although this was not a surrogate for all urban in-migration, it may have been representative of the movement of young, single people, who formed the most dynamic component of the migration stream. Analysis of apprenticeship migration to Edinburgh in the seventeenth century has shown that the capital drew recruits from throughout Scotland. The far-flung activities of Edinburgh's merchants encouraged an unusually wide pattern of recruitment. There was a marked distance-decay effect, with a high proportion of migrant apprentices originating from areas close to the city. Patterns of movement varied from trade to trade; the low status of weavers was reflected in recruitment from a purely local hinterland while the high-status goldsmiths were drawn from a much wider area. There were marked differences in the numbers of apprentices moving to Edinburgh from particular regions, once the size of their populations and their distance from the capital is allowed for. In the late seventeenth century the lightly urbanised south east of Scotland sent disproportionately more apprentices to Edinburgh, as did Aberdeenshire, probably due to links generated through coastal trade. On the other hand Fife, Perthshire, Angus and Kincardine provided proportionally fewer apprentices than other regions, possibly due to the existence of local opportunities for prospective apprentices in the many small burghs of Fife, and in Dundee and Perth (Lovett *et al.*, 1985).

In the seventeenth century the pull of Glasgow was not yet strong enough to check the flow of apprentices from west-central Scotland. Glasgow drew apprentices from only a limited area; Lanarkshire, Renfrewshire and Dunbartonshire provided 77 per cent of migrant apprentices between 1625 and 1649. Few Glasgow apprentices came from Ayrshire, Galloway or the west Highlands. Migration to Aberdeen and Inverness was likewise markedly regional in character, over 75 per cent coming from within a 40 km radius of each town.

Similar patterns of movement are evident for women moving to Scottish towns, as revealed by marriage registers (Whyte and Whyte, 1988). Of women migrating to Edinburgh before marriage in the first decade of the eighteenth century 38 per cent came from within the Lothians, 19 per cent from Fife and 11 per cent from the Borders but significant numbers came from further afield, including the Highlands, the Northern Isles and England. Smaller towns like Haddington or Prestonpans drew 60–70 per cent of marriage partners from within the parish and most of the remainder from a radius of 12–15 km (Whyte, 1987).

Students were another group of temporary residents in the university towns of St Andrews, Aberdeen, Glasgow and Edinburgh. Although their numbers were small for most of the early-modern period – *c.*200 in Aberdeen in the mid-seventeenth century – there were as many as 1,000 in Edinburgh at the start of the eighteenth century. Edinburgh was also noted for its provision of secondary education. In the late sixteenth century many Border lairds were sending their sons to the High School and a century later it was fashionable for landowners to send their daughters to finishing schools in the capital. Another distinctive component of urban in-migration was the settlement of Highlanders. They were present in only small numbers in Scottish towns during the sixteenth and early seventeenth centuries but sufficiently numerous to form distinctive communities in towns like Edinburgh and Stirling by the later seventeenth century (Withers, 1985). Highland migrants were mostly poor and frequently spoke little English. They tended to take unskilled jobs as porters and chairmen, or combined small-scale retailing with begging. By the early eighteenth century most of the larger towns are likely to have had a Highland element in their population.

The poor who, as in England, may have accounted for 30–40 per cent of the population of larger Scottish towns are even less well recorded than their southern counterparts. It has been suggested that there may not have been the same widespread immigration of rural population into Scottish towns in the sixteenth century as there was in England. However, the policy adopted by the councils of larger towns of keeping food prices low rather than paying poor relief might have served to encourage rather than discourage such movement. It is likely that then, as later, there was a steady flow of vagrants into the towns, competing with the urban poor for charity. A distinction was drawn in towns between people considered 'indwellers' by virtue of birth, parentage or, less certainly, length of residence and those who were 'outland' folk. The repetition of acts of burgh courts requiring the expulsion of 'stranger beggars' merely serves to underline the problems of identifying incomers, many of whom were able to stay in suburbs beyond the control of urban authorities. To this steady flow from town to country was added waves of desperate people during subsistence crises like 1580, 1622–23 or the later 1690s. In Edinburgh in the 1690s the council set up a relief camp for starving vagrants in the Greyfriars Churchyard. In Aberdeen in February 1696 the authorities attempted to expel all beggars who had entered the town in search of food and set guards on the gates to prevent any more from gaining admittance.

There must also have been a counter-current of people moving back to the countryside, although this is harder to identify. This would have included apprentices who had served their time and female domestic servants returning home to marry. In the 1690s the four largest Scottish towns are likely to have employed around 12,000 female domestic servants. This reverse movement must also have involved a significant flow of money from town to countryside in the form of remittances and savings.

Industrial Specialization in Towns and their Hinterlands

A notable feature of Scottish towns, particularly in the sixteenth century, was the limited range of industrial and craft activities that were carried out in most of them. This was due to the importance of overseas trade even in the smallest royal burghs. Virtually every royal burgh, whether port or inland town, depended to some extent on the export of staple commodities: wool, skins, hides, cloth, fish, salt and coal. This made them vulnerable to variations in both local supply and overseas demand. Dependence on exports of raw materials from predominantly agricultural hinterlands was matched by reliance on imported manufactures, which restricted, to a degree unusual in northern Europe, the range of occupations in many Scottish towns well into the seventeenth century. English visitors were struck by the lack of industry in even the larger towns in the later sixteenth century. The smallness of the textile sector was a distinctive feature of Scottish towns in general, with the partial exception of Dundee, unlike England where it was a major source of urban wealth.

The occupational structure of Scottish towns was neither unchanging over time nor completely uniform. During the fifteenth and sixteenth centuries, as patterns of trade changed, Scottish towns slowly began to diversify their economic activities. By the early sixteenth century each of the four main towns had developed distinctive occupational structures. Perth was very much a craft town where the trades incorporations paid as much tax as the merchants who focused on inland rather than overseas trade. There was a narrower gap in wealth between craftsman and merchant in Perth than in other large towns and a correspondingly high proportion of craftsmen joining the merchant guild – 44 per cent of entrants in the 1560s. Perth was dominated by manufacturing but nevertheless had only a small textile sector. Glasgow in the sixteenth century was still a town dependent on internal rather than overseas trade with a relatively broad manufacturing base. The city's population began to rise before the late seventeenth century but in the 1630s Glasgow was still a town with a relatively under-developed economy in relation to its size, a regional centre relying mainly on inland trade with a modest merchant community but an unusually broad manufacturing base, especially in textiles, clothing and food processing (Lynch, 1987).

Dundee was oriented towards exports to a much greater degree and specialised more in cloth production than did any other major town. A narrower range of manufacturing than Perth and a more limited spectrum of overseas trade than Edinburgh made Dundee especially vulnerable to shifts in internal supply and external demand. Aberdeen, dominated by trade rather than manufacture, drew on the produce of a more extensive rural hinterland than did other regional centres. The town's relative slippage during the seventeenth century may have been due less to the conservative practices of its merchants than to the fact that the town's hinterland had a more limited range of activities than those towns in the Central Lowlands. Aberdeen had proportionally more merchants than Edinburgh and fewer craftsmen. Edinburgh specialised in the finishing and luxury trades to a greater degree than the other large towns but had a much greater overseas trading base.

The late sixteenth/early seventeenth-century expansion of trade may have led to some diversification into a wider range of exports. In Aberdeen increasing amounts of wool were woven into plaiding, which led to the introduction of dyeing and the manufacture of stockings. The export of hides ceased around 1600 as they were made into leather and from 1629 the leather began to be exported as gloves. In addition there was a marked rise in exports of fish and grain in the first three decades of the seventeenth century. Some of the profits from this went into financing a range of public works in the town. The impact of this phase of prosperity on other regional centres has yet to be considered in detail (Macniven, 1977).

Sixteenth-century tax rolls show repeated fluctuations in the proportions of taxation paid by particular towns. Perth's assessment rose three times and fell seven times between 1550 and 1635 while Glasgow's rose six times and fell three (Lynch, 1987). This suggests recurrent short-term crises in many towns due to fluctuations in overseas trade and increasing competition for declining overseas markets as Edinburgh increased its hold over foreign trade. The effect of such crises on population, society and economy still remains to be studied. The decay of many medium-sized towns continued through the sixteenth century, despite the improvement in trade, due to the rise of Edinburgh. Middle-rank towns and larger regional centres may have been forced more into coastal trade feeding Leith. There was a general gain of inland trade by the larger regional centres at the expense of smaller ones by the end of the sixteenth century. Between 1535 and 1635 the tax rolls show the dominant position of Edinburgh, which was consolidated throughout the period. The large regional centres, like some in England, also consolidated their position in relation to smaller towns in their regions. Edinburgh in the 1590s had a complete monopoly on the export of raw wool, 83 per cent of the exported hides and 76 per cent of the woollen cloth.

The distribution of large-scale textile production in the seventeenth and early eighteenth centuries emphasises the importance of larger burghs as centres for financing, organising and marketing rural textiles. Woollens (plaiding and stockings) were important around Aberdeen in the first half of the seventeenth century, linen around Glasgow and Dundee. Many of the industrial occupations in Scottish towns until well into the seventeenth century were geared to the finishing or part finishing of commodities from their rural hinterlands for the export market. Royal burgh monopolies bound towns to their hinterlands rather than set them apart. Town and country fed on each other for materials, labour and capital. Rather than town and countryside being sharply defined and distinctive there was regular contact between the two and a high turnover of people. Travelling merchants, packmen and chapmen carried urban manufactures and imports to the countryside. The privileges of the royal burghs actually encouraged rural dwellers to frequent urban markets by imposing restrictions on the development of putting-out systems. The Aberdeen Dean of Guild court forbade merchants to buy cloth direct from rural manufacturers. The cloth had to be inspected and stamped before being sold in fairs or markets. The predominance of the kaufsystem, whereby individual weavers sold their webs of cloth to travelling merchants at fairs, brought rural people into the towns (Tyson, 1989).

The huge expansion of Aberdeen's export trade in plaiding in the early seventeenth century was based on merchants purchasing the cloth from independent weavers rather than using putting-out systems as Aberdeen merchants were forbidden to send wool out to the countryside to be woven. Exports of plaiding rose from *c*.13,000 ells a year at the start of the seventeenth century to 121,000 in 1639. Most of the production was located in the countryside and in 1624 it was estimated that *c*.20,000 people in the North East earned their living from the manufacture of plaiding.

In the first half of the seventeenth century new manufactories developed in the suburbs or hinterlands of Edinburgh, mainly financed by merchant capital like the Newmills cloth manufactory at Haddington. The same period saw the flight of some crafts to the suburbs and the growth of satellite towns, often with specialised workforces. In the later seventeenth century a number of manufactories for a range of products, especially textiles, was established in central Scotland, financed largely by capital from the mercantile and professional élites of Edinburgh and Glasgow. The growth of towns in the central belt of Scotland also had a significant effect on the coal mining industry. Although substantial quanties of coal were exported, and used in salt manufacture, domestic consumption, much of it in the towns, was also a major consumer.

Towns as Social Centres

Town and country were linked by careers and intermarriage. Apprenticeship to a merchant was a common career outlet for younger sons of lairds. Intermarriage between urban élites and landowning families was also frequent. Studies of the social structures of larger Scottish towns at this period sometimes imply that the urban population was made up entirely of merchants, craftsmen, servants, labourers and their families, ignoring the professions. It has been suggested that 'shire towns' or sheriffdom centres had a much less important function in Scotland than in England because so much justice was devolved to rural franchise courts while diocesan centres were not significant unless they were also university towns like St Andrews and Glasgow. Nevertheless, before the Reformation, the area occupied by the cathedral canons formed a distinctive area within larger diocesan centres like Glasgow and smaller ones like Dunkeld.

The role of Scottish towns as administrative and service centres for the surrounding countryside has probably been underestimated. In the early sixteenth century North East landed families made considerable use of Aberdeen-based notaries to carry out legal work relating to their estates. A recent study of Elgin has demonstrated that in this small, inland town with a population of only 2,000–2,500, and a relatively poor merchant community, the legal profession was important in terms of both wealth and political power (Thomas, 1993). In the mid-seventeenth century between 10 and 20 notaries were active in the town at any time. They paid more per head in taxation than the merchants and all but the wealthiest craftsmen and occupied up to 30 per cent of the seats on the burgh council. Like their Edinburgh counterparts some were affluent enough to purchase estates. Elgin was not the only inland burgh with only a modest amount of overseas trade and it would be surprising if it were unique in terms of the role of its legal profession.

It was common for landowners to have town houses in regional centres like Aberdeen and Perth. By the late seventeenth century Perth functioned as a winter leisure centre for landowners from the central Highlands, suitably equipped with numerous inns and brothels. Stirling and Edinburgh attracted the nobility in the sixteenth century due to the presence of the court. After 1603 and the removal of the court to London the expansion of central legal and administrative functions in Edinburgh perpetuated its role as a centre for landed society. Landowners formed a significant group in Edinburgh society in the 1690s, including those who owned town houses and those who occupied rented accommodation (Dingwall, 1994). Many men listed as advocates were also landowners. By the end of the seventeenth century, however, cramped conditions in the town centre were encouraging some landowners to move outside Edinburgh and build mansions in the suburbs.

There was a decisive shift in Edinburgh's functions after the middle of the seventeenth century. The capital no longer had a virtual monopoly entrepôt trade; its economy shifted towards that of an administrative and social centre with a marked concentration in the professions and the service sector (Lynch, 1991). By 1694 the professions, principally the lawyers, paid 34 per cent of Edinburgh's tax, more than the merchants and craftsmen combined. The lawyers were an important bridge between town and country. Although Edinburgh's flowering as a cultural centre lay in the later eighteenth century its origins began in the sevententh, especially after the Restoration. In the late seventeenth century there was an increase in book publishing in the city. The first provincial newspapers appeared and the city's role as a postal centre grew. The university had *c*.1,000 students by 1700 but the town was also noted as a centre for secondary education; as well as the prestigious High School there was an increasing number of educational establishments, including finishing schools for girls, which encouraged the landed élite to send their daughters to the capital (Houston, 1993). The patronage of the Duke of York was important in encouraging many aspects of the sciences, not only by aristocratic dilettantes but increasingly by Edinburgh-based lawyers and doctors, foreshadowing the middle-class character of the eighteenth-century Enlightenment (Chapter 3).

Other large towns functioned as social centres at a regional scale. In the early sixteenth century it was almost a token of social status for landed families in north east Scotland to have a town house in Aberdeen. Even in the early sixteenth century demand for luxury items in the rural hinterland of this relatively remote town was sufficient to keep several goldsmiths in employment. Legal work provided a lucrative income for notaries, some of whom joined the merchant guild, were active in burgh politics and purchased urban property. The resident heritors in the later seventeenth century were mainly small lairds, many of them from cadet branches of ubiquitous north-eastern families like Forbes and Gordon, living off rents of under £500 Scots a year. Smaller towns also had significant social roles. Old Aberdeen had a disproportionately high number of lairds and gentry.

* * *

By the mid-eighteenth century the range of industrial, commercial and social activities in Scotland's larger towns was broadening as the economy itself became more complex, and many of these new activities were starting to percolate downwards to lower levels of the urban hierarchy. Scotland, although still an overwhelmingly rural country, had by 1760 one of the fastest-growing urban sectors in Europe, one poised for the dramatic expansion which would, within three generations, turn Scotland into a predominantly urban society.

7

ECONOMIC DECLINE AND GROWTH

The economic history of early-modern Scotland has not received as much attention in recent years as its social history. The standard works on the Scottish economy remain those of Lythe (1963) for the late sixteenth and early seventeenth century, and Smout (1963) for the later seventeenth century. There is a need for a reassessment of the broad pattern of Scotland's economic development in the two centuries before the start of the Industrial Revolution. There is also plenty of scope for more detailed work, particularly research focusing on periods that fall between those covered by the two seminal works mentioned above, the middle decades of the seventeenth century and the years following the Union of 1707. Nevertheless, in the last two decades there have been important advances in our knowledge of many aspects of Scotland's economic development, notably agriculture and the trends of prices and wages. We also have a far clearer picture of urban development, especially the economic activities of mercantile élites, and urban occupational structures. Moreover, there has been important work on specific industries such as coal, salt production and textiles.

Economic Growth: The Later Sixteenth and Early Seventeenth Centuries

In surveying the Scottish economy from 1500 to the mid-eighteenth century continuity is often more apparent than change, poverty more evident than prosperity. Throughout most of the period Scotland remained a peripheral and backward country in European terms. In 1500, 1600 and even in great measure 1700

Scotland retained an economic structure that was essentially medieval, resting on the primary products of agriculture, fishing and mining, along with a limited range of low-grade manufactures like linen and woollen cloth. In return Scotland imported a wide range of manufactures and luxury items as well as basic raw materials like iron and timber.

At a time when the horizons of European traders were widening to include the New World, Africa and the East Indies, those of Scottish merchants were firmly fixed on more local waters. Scotland's pattern of trade remained stubbornly conservative, centred around the North Sea using tried and tested markets, which reduced the element of risk to merchants whose resources were generally limited. One or two Scottish voyages to the Mediterranean are recorded in the early seventeenth century but there are few other signs of a wider outlook. In the sixteenth and early seventeenth centuries the most notable changes were the relative decline in trade with France, especially following the Reformation and the Union of 1603, the continuing importance and growth of trade with the Low Countries, and the steady rise of England as a trading partner. Trade with Ireland, easily overlooked, provided a valuable boost to west-coast burghs, particularly after the Ulster plantations in the early seventeenth century.

Although the evidence for economic change in the sixteenth century is fragmentary the overall trends are clear. From a low level early in the century Scottish trade expanded in the 1530s, slumped again during the English invasions of the 1540s, then grew more steadily during the second half of the century to reach a peak during the 1620s and early 1630s (Guy, 1986). Economic growth in the later sixteenth century took place against a background of rapid inflation. Inflation and economic growth were partly fuelled by population increase. The scale of demographic expansion in the sixteenth century can only be guessed at but a 50 per cent rise has been suggested. As population grew, poverty widened to include not just the aged and infirm but whole sections of the population. The economy was not expanding fast enough to absorb the surplus labour. Able bodied vagrants were seen as a major social problem as the concept of unemployment was not recognised and it was assumed by the authorities that such people would not rather than could not find work.

There was a rapid rise in coal exports from the 1590s, paralleled by the growth of the salt industry. Coal exports in the 1570s and 80s at times reached 5,000 tons a year. In 1614 they stood at *c.*15,000 tons, and in the decade after 1621 *c.*25,000 tons, coastal traffic as well as exports, was shipped from the Forth. Production of lead ore followed a similar trend. Indirect indicators of an expansion in industrial output is suggested by rising imports of flax iron and timber. Shipments of iron from the Baltic more than trebled between the 1570s and the 1630s while those of flax and hemp doubled (Lythe, 1963).

The discovery of various metallic ores stimulated a wave of prospecting and mining in the Lowlands. The Scottish crown was perennially short of bullion and the discovery of gold in upper Clydesdale was especially welcome. Lead mining was also beginning to make a useful contribution to Scottish exports by the early seventeenth century. In 1611–14 the value of lead ore exported nearly equalled that of coal and was almost twice that of linen. Although small-scale working at a number of sites including Islay and Lismore produced a fluctuating output the principal mining field lay around Leadhills on the watershed between Clydesdale and Nithsdale. Some lead had been mined there in the later sixteenth century. In 1638 the mines came into the possession of Sir James Hope and production was stepped up. By the mid-seventeenth century some 50 workers were producing 3–400 tons of ore a year. Most of it was exported unprocessed to the Low Countries due to the difficulty of obtaining fuel for smelting on site.

The Scottish iron industry was hampered by a lack of suitable ore as well as fuel. High-grade haematite occurred in only a few localities and although the clayband ores of the Carboniferous strata were first used in the early seventeenth century, the richer blackband ores were not exploited until much later. This explains the substantial imports of Swedish iron. There was still timber in the Highlands where bog ore was widely smelted in small quantities using primitive bloomery forges. Possibilities for developing larger charcoal blast-furnaces in the Highlands were being considered in the early seventeenth century. This prompted an Act of Parliament in 1609 forbidding the setting up of 'yrne mylnes' in the region to prevent the destruction of woodlands.

Sir George Hay, one of the 'adventurers' who had made abortive attempts to settle a colony of Lowlanders in Lewis, appears to have done a deal with Mackenzie of Kintail in which, in return for transferring all his rights in Lewis, Hay got access to woods around Loch Maree. He used his influence at court to obtain an exemption from the 1609 act and by 1610 a blast-furnace, the first in Scotland, was operating on the shores of the loch, aided by English technology and possibly English capital. In a pattern that was to become a model for later industrial developments in the Highlands skilled workers were brought in from north west England. Cumbrian haematite and clayband ore from Fife were shipped to Poolewe. The history of the venture is obscure but the smelter still seems to have been operating in 1626. Hay's scheme, surprisingly successful in its day, was nevertheless ahead of its time. It was not until the early eighteenth century, when the Highlands were more settled, that further large-scale ironmaking ventures were undertaken there.

Less glamorous than the hunt for gold and silver but more important for the economy was the mining of coal. Coal had been worked in Scotland in medieval times but only on a small scale. The later sixteenth and early seventeenth centuries saw a major increase in production. Mining technology remained primitive: most mines were small, the coal being worked from surface outcrops or by shallow bell pits and levels. Nevertheless, by the early seventeenth century improved technology from England and Flanders was being applied at some collieries allowing deeper working. The most famous example was Sir George Bruce's mine at Culross, one of the wonders of its day. Before Bruce took over the colliery in 1575 it had been worked to a shallow depth by Cistercian monks and then abandoned due to drainage difficulties. Bruce had the mine extended nearly a mile under the Firth of Forth. Problems of drainage and ventilation were tackled by horse-driven pumps and by the ambitious scheme of sinking a shaft from an artificial island at the lowest level of the foreshore. At high tide the top of the shaft was surrounded by the sea, allowing the coal to be wound up and loaded directly on to vessels moored at an adjacent pier. The mine was linked to 44 salt pans, making it one of the largest integrated industrial units in Scotland.

Large collieries are also recorded from the upper Forth around Alloa in the early seventeenth century, some of them financed by Edinburgh merchant capital. Exports of coal are thought to have risen substantially from the later sixteenth century. In the 1570s and 80s exports at times reached around 5,000 tons a year. By 1614 the figure was around 15,000 tons rising to over 70,000 tons for a brief period in the 1660s. Export duties on English coal from 1599 helped to make Scottish coal competitive abroad and it also began to find a market in England, especially London.

Closely linked to the expansion of coal mining was the development of the salt industry. In the sixteenth century Scotland imported a good deal of French salt but the dislocation of this trade stimulated production at home while exports of Scottish salt to the Baltic and the Low Countries also rose. The dross from the coal mines was used for evaporating sea water in large shallow iron pans to produce sea salt. Salt making was widespread around the shores of the Forth. Scottish salt exports were only a tiny fraction of the European trade but Scottish producers were quick to take advantage of market opportunities. The collapse of the Dutch salt trade with Spain as a result of the outbreak of the Dutch Revolt in 1566 created conditions that gave Scottish high-cost, low-quality producers a chance to increase their exports. The volume of salt exported increased eight times in the early 1570s. Generally favourable conditions for export continued until the early 1640s.

Scotland was richly endowed with fisheries but not with the resources to exploit them effectively. Much fishing was a supplementary rather than a specialised activity. Salmon formed a useful source of additional income on many estates, the Tweed, Tay and Dee being particularly important. In 1614 salmon accounted for about a third of the value of fish exported from Scotland, the rest being mainly herring. The Scots were disadvantaged in the herring fishery compared with the Dutch by their lack of capital. In 1594 the Dutch had been granted access to Scottish waters provided that they did not fish close inshore. Their large, efficiently organised fleet, complete with storeships and warships for protection, was seen as a model to emulate. The Scottish fishing industry remained local and small scale, depending on open boats operating close to the shore. Such vessels brought their summers' catches to centres like Anstruther, Crail, Dunbar or Greenock for salting and sale. The main exceptions were the Clyde herring fishermen who operated in West Highland waters with a fleet of hundreds of boats.

Peace and political stability under James VI was probably the most significant contribution of a king whose interest in, and grasp of, economic matters was notoriously limited and whose attitude to merchants verged on the contemptuous. The expansion of trade and economic growth in the later sixteenth centuriy occurred without the support of any coherent government policy, mercantilist or otherwise. Economic legislation lacked direction and often demonstrated a failure to understand how the economy worked. The government blew hot and cold on the export of wool and the import of cloth depending on customs receipts and which pressure group – the Convention or major landowners – shouted loudest. Governments tried to protect consumers rather than encouraging merchants. Exports were regulated more closely than imports for these were more sensitive when grain, cattle and fish were vital to subsistence and coal, salt and wool were also needed at home. Official action worked best in short-term crises, grappling with the problem of famine by banning grain exports, prohibiting hoarding and imposing price controls. Governments did not intervene in agriculture other than attempting to control the supply of grain in the short term during periods of dearth. They were, however, more concerned to regulate fisheries, particularly salmon (Goodare, 1989).

After 1603 James gradually relinquished decision making on economic matters to the Privy Council. They still did not have a clear policy but there was a gradual move away from the traditional outlook of the king towards one which favoured merchants and producers as well as offering protection to consumers. The Privy Council deserves much of the credit for creating a favourable economic climate in the early seventeenth century, supporting the burghs and encouraging the economic interests of landowners.

Industrial growth occurred in spite of rather than because of official encouragement, which relied mainly on the granting of monopolies to individuals. Some 24 attempts to establish manufactures or purchase monopolies are recorded between 1587 and 1642, ranging from paper and pottery to glass and gunpowder, soap and sugar. Production seems to have been short lived and of little consequence in most cases. Sir George Hay's glassworks at Wemyss and Nathaniel Udward's soapworks at Leith were more successful than most. With protection from competition Hay's glassworks flourished and by 1625 was exporting drinking glasses to London in some quantity. Initiative regarding industrial policy still lay largely with the Convention, whose attitude was conservative and rigid, more concerned to maintain traditional privileges and resist competition than to innovate. Efforts to improve the quality of woollens by importing foreign workers failed, although the traditional woollen industry expanded in the 1620s.

It can be questioned how widely the profits of economic growth during this period were spread beyond the urban, and to some degree the landed, élites. Dodgshon (1981) has characterised the economy of late sixteenth-century Scotland as one of growing contrast between increasingly prosperous towns and an impoverished countryside. The picture may not have been too different in the early seventeenth century. Despite the expansion of trade and industry it would be dangerously optimistic to talk of a transformation of the Scottish economy in the late sixteenth and early seventeenth centuries. Increases in production in industries like coal and salt were often spectacular in proportional terms but started from very low baselines. One cannot even talk about an 'industrial sector' in an economy that was still so overwhelmingly agrarian (Devine and Lythe, 1971). Most coal mines and salt works were still adjuncts to estates where the bulk of the income came from agriculture.

The Union of 1603 did not mark a major watershed in economic relations between Scotland and England, merely a further stage in a slow process of integration. One solid result of the Union, the pacification of the Borders, allowed livestock farmers in this region to turn to commercial livestock production. The Union, however, also involved costs for Scotland; ties with France were loosened while incomes that might have been spent in Scotland were drawn to London. James VI was keen on promoting a full economic union between the two countries but this was unacceptable to the English Parliament and was not welcomed north of the Border either.

Opposition to the idea of free trade between the two countries came mainly from England. Rational economic debate was submerged by national prejudice. The English feared that the Scots would undercut them in both manufacturing and trade – Scottish labour costs were certainly lower – and unleash on England a plague of poor pedlars. Scotland would gain access to the wealth of England, providing only poor fish and worse cloth in return. English grain would flow north, bringing dearth in the south. Overall the incentives for economic union were not great. After 1603 the Scots traded with England on terms that were slightly more favourable than before – they had the benefit of being exempt from the additional customs tax on aliens – while English merchants could trade in Scotland without payment of some customs duties. Scots born after 1603 were only given full rights in England after James had agreed not to give his countrymen undue preferment to offices in England (Galloway, 1986).

Charles I aimed at a closer integration of the Scottish and English economies under umbrella mercantilist policies. This was seen most clearly in his efforts to set up a common fishery within Scotland, England and Ireland in 1630 to emulate and replace the Dutch. Scottish fishermen from Lowland ports were only just beginning to exploit the rich fisheries off the Western Isles when the Dutch began to fish the area regularly in the 1620s. Colin Mackenzie, first Earl of Seaforth, was keen to cash in on the Dutch activities by developing Stornoway as a base for them. This brought the Dutch inshore, where they came into competition with the Scots.

Charles' plan was for an organisation of provincial fishing associations around the British Isles, raising investment locally but regulated overall by a council, a structure closely following the one operated by the Dutch. The plan for a fleet of 200 herring busses, deep water vessels of 30–50 tons, involved a massive amount of capital. However, the scheme was tied to English rather than Scottish economic policy and the Scots saw in it, probably correctly, the threat of English vessels invading Scottish waters. Anglo-Scottish discussions about the common fishery became increasingly acrimonious as the Scots commissioners saw a threat to their national identity. The English commissioners were more willing to make concessions to the Scots than Charles was and the scheme collapsed (Macinnes, 1991).

Recent work has suggested that the scale and impact of economic growth in late sixteenth- and especially early seventeenth-century Scotland was greater than has previously been appreciated. This has been highlighted by Brown's (1985) study of the activities of Edinburgh's merchant élite. In the later sixteenth and early seventeenth centuries the domination of Edinburgh over Scottish trade was even greater than that of London over English commerce. As early as 1480 Edinburgh had accounted for 54 per cent of Scotland's export revenues. By 1578 this had risen to 75 per cent. Over the period 1460–1600 Edinburgh handled the export of 76 per cent of Scotland's wool, 73 per cent of the cloth, 80 per cent of the sheepskins, 83 per cent of the hides and much of the trade in fish, hosiery, plaiding and grain (Lynch, 1987). During the first four decades of the seventeenth century more and more of Scotland's trade came into the hands of a small élite of Edinburgh merchants. Their business methods became increasingly sophisticated, involving the use of joint-stock companies, especially for imports where the element of risk was greatest, and the employment of factors in foreign cities providing rudimentary banking services. It was formerly believed that such practices were first introduced by Scottish merchants in the later seventeenth century, transforming the antiquated trading system and forming an essential foundation for economic development in the eighteenth century. It is now clear that such methods were already in use half a century earlier.

As their wealth increased Edinburgh's élite diversified into new enterprises. They became increasingly active as shipowners. Vessels, or shares in ships, accounted for 26 per cent of the value of their inventories. Patrick Wood, who died in 1638, owned shares in at least 36 vessels, although these assets accounted for only 16 per cent of the total value of his inventory. Some merchants speculated in grain futures by the advance purchase of crops for agreed sums. Of more general importance was their investment in industry including lead mining, coal and salt production, herring curing, brewing, rope making and cloth manufacture. Several merchants owned salt pans around the Forth and the boom in salt production in the early seventeenth century may have been due to injections of Edinburgh merchant capital. A herring curing factory in Dunbar, which had come into the hands of William Dick, greatest of Edinburgh's merchant princes, was valued at 60,000 merks in 1642. In 1597, 18 Edinburgh merchants set up the Society of Brewers, whose plant was worth 40,000 merks in 1618. It too was taken over by Dick, who also had a soapworks in Leith (Brown, 1985).

Edinburgh's wealthiest merchants derived an increasing proportion of their income from money-lending in the 1620s and 30s. Over half the city's richest merchants were involved in money-lending as an integral part of their activities. Another outlet for Edinburgh merchant capital was investment in urban property. Population growth in the city encouraged a boom in tenement construction, especially in the 1630s, financed by richer merchants, of which Gladstone's Land in the Lawnmarket is a surviving example. By 1635 over half the city's wealthier merchants were profiting from urban property.

Edinburgh's merchant élite also invested in rural property. This did not normally involve the purchase of estates with the aim of increasing their social status. It was done mainly for business purposes. Much of the money that they lent was on wadset, giving them control of land and its products in lieu of interest. It has been suggested, on the strength of the limited mercantile involvement in land during the later seventeenth century, that Scottish merchants had little interest in rural property. From the 1590s, however, their activities in this sector expanded rapidly. In the charters of the Register of the Great Seal for the early decades of the seventeenth century 60 per cent of the transactions involved merchants, the bulk of them from Edinburgh.

Involvement in land by Edinburgh merchants in the early seventeenth century was spread throughout Scotland: 36 per cent of transactions concerned land in the Lothians, 13 per cent in Fife, 13 per cent in west-central Scotland, 14 per cent in the south west, 14 per cent north of the Tay and 10 per cent in the Borders. There was a concentration on arable areas, suggesting links with the grain trade, much of which was in the hands of the élite. Although merchants were not directly involved in crop production, it is possible that their capital lay behind the mini agricultural revolution in the Lothians in the early seventeenth century, with the widespread adoption of liming and substantial increases in both crop yields and rents (Chapter 6).

Disaster, Recovery and Crisis

The economic boom that saw the rise of Edinburgh's merchant élite was ending by the mid-1630s. When Charles I visited Scotland in 1633 he was greeted with complaints about the decay of towns and trade. Athough recession was already starting to bite, the outbreak of the Covenanting Wars in 1638 was a disaster of major proportions whose full effects on the economy have yet to be properly assessed. The 1640s and 50s have been treated by historians primarily in political and social rather than economic terms. It is almost as though the economy was put on hold in 1638 only to re-emerge in a very shaky condition in the later years of Cromwell's rule. Yet through all the campaigns of these disturbed decades crops continued to be sown and harvested, markets and fairs held, goods imported and exported.

After the Restoration a reaction set in as the Scots tried to blot out the memory of this traumatic period of disruption, so that the idea that the Covenanting period contributed anything positive to Scottish economic development might seem unlikely. A thorough study of the economic context of this period is overdue. Stevenson (1988) has looked at the Covenanting regime and found examples of forward-looking economic policies that survived the Restoration. Acts passed by Parliament during the Covenanting period for encouraging manufactures and agricultural improvement, although axed by the Act Recissory in 1661, were subsequently revived. An Act of Parliament in 1641 was designed to encourage the manufacture of fine woollens by freeing foreign wool and dyestuffs from import duties and removing taxes on the cloth that was produced. Manufactories were started at Bonnington near Edinburgh, at Ayr and at Newmills near Haddington. They seem to have enjoyed modest success but they faced the problems that blighted all attempts to develop high-quality textile production in seventeenth-century Scotland: high costs, lack of a skilled workforce, insufficient capital and a limited home market.

During the Restoration period there appears to have been a marked change of attitude on the part of Scottish landowners towards their tenants and estates, away from traditional concepts of feudal lordship and towards more commercial goals. One possible outcome of this – although the actual mechanisms are not clear – was a marked improvement in food supply, accompanied by a fall in prices. In the later seventeenth century significant harvest failures only occurred in 1674 and the later 1690s. In the first half of the eighteenth century 1709, 1724–25 and 1740–41 were years of shortage but not of major mortality crises. This contrasts markedly with the frequency of famine in the late sixteenth century. Between 1560 and 1600 it has been estimated by Lythe (1963) that in one year in three there was dearth in at least some part of Scotland. Slackening of demographic pressure may have been an influence behind the improved food supply. Greater efficiency in agriculture and estate management along with better marketing are other possibilities. Given the modest level of crop yields of traditional Scottish infield–outfield farming even a marginal improvement could have been significant in increasing the supply of grain. The famines of the later 1690s came as a shock after 35 years of generally abundant basic food supplies and low prices. They did not recur, however, and were in many respects an aberration. In the first 40 years of the eighteenth century improved poor relief undoubtedly helped the weaker sectors of society in years of shortage.

Low grain prices and limited opportunities to accumulate capital made agricultural improvement a poor investment and ensured that any experiments in this direction were confined to the parks and home farms of estates (Whyte, 1979). Low prices may also have forced many bonnet lairds to sell out and they did nothing to help small farmers whose meagre surpluses could generate little cash. This may have encouraged them to adopt industrial by-employments. Low food prices must have benefited urban wage-earners, although it is not clear whether the combination of steady wages and low food prices allowed any significant accumulation of urban capital among a wide range of people.

Economic recovery after the Restoration was slow. The Dutch wars of 1665–67 and 1672–74 were setbacks to progress while the English Navigation Act, which contravened the rights of naturalisation that had been agreed for Scots in 1608, hampered Anglo-Scottish trade. It it unlikely that economic recovery was sufficient to restore the level of prosperity reached in the 1630s but the scale of expansion was nevertheless considerable. The 1670s especially were a boom period, marked by a great increase in the volume of shipping as merchants and skippers took advantage of the opportunities offered by British neutrality amidst European conflict. The 1680s were less prosperous. Higher tariffs on Scottish grain and coal caused problems as Scotland's trading partners, notably France, adopted increasingly protectionist policies. Plaiding lost most of its established markets in France, Sweden and Holland in the late 1680s and early 1690s.

The stubbornly conservative pattern of trade in the later seventeenth century confirmed the fears of many who were concerned about Scotland's long-term economic development. In such a poor country the domestic market was limited and could not be expanded rapidly. As a result prosperity depended on developing and retaining overseas markets. The increasing difficulties faced by the Scottish economy in the later seventeenth century were partly due to the fact that while foreign trade was vital to Scotland its contribution in European terms was marginal.

Scottish merchants were small-scale operators by European standards and no Scottish merchant in the Restoration period could match the scale and diversity of operations of Edinburgh's merchant princes of the pre-Covenanting era. Memories of their dramatic downfall may have cautioned their successors against overexpansion. Yet it was from these seventeenth-century merchants that the increasingly successful Scottish business class of the eighteenth century was to evolve. Before criticising them too severely for lack of enterprise and vision it is worth reflecting that, compared with Irish merchants at this time, Scottish traders displayed greater flexibility and business acumen. A reassessment of late seventeenth-century Glasgow merchants is similarly positive (Devine and Jackson, 1995).

Enterprise was not confined to the merchant class. In the later seventeenth century many landowners were also active in trade and industry. Given the sluggish prices for grain the diversification of estate economies was a sensible approach. Proprietors in Galloway and the more accessible areas of the Highlands were involved in cattle droving. East-coast landowners from East Lothian to the Moray Firth and beyond handled grain, sometimes shipping it directly abroad when prices at home were low. Proprietors around the Forth develped coal mines and salt works on an increasingly large scale.

Although quantities are elusive, Scotland's main exports in the late seventeenth century can be ranked approximately by value. There were some major changes from the early part of the century when hides and skins, followed by herring, linen and woollen cloth, had been the most valuable exports. Linen now occupied the first place followed by cattle and wool (during those periods when the export of wool was permitted), with coal, salt, fish, woollens and grain of lesser importance but still significant. Voyages to Iberia were no more frequent than they had been earlier in the century but ventures to the Canaries and Madeira by Glasgow ships were a new development during the 1690s. Trade with England after 1660 was handicapped by the English Navigation Act and by substantial tariffs on many commodities, notably coal, linen, salt and cattle. By the end of the century tobacco was one of the most valuable imports from England: over 2 million pounds in 1700. Although linen was Scotland's most prominent export to England a good deal of finer cloth came north in return (Smout, 1963).

An important development in the later seventeenth century was the start of trans-Atlantic trade by Glasgow merchants. In 1656 Thomas Tucker noted that Glasgow vessels had already ventured to the West Indies. By the 1680s a number of vessels were trading with the Caribbean and the North American mainland. This contravened the English Navigation Act but the Scottish Privy Council seem to have turned a blind eye. Between 1680 and 1686 over 40 voyages to the New World are recorded. Sugar and tobacco were the main imports, with linen and woollen cloth, yarn, hosiery, shoes and hardware among the exports. The dynamic approach of the Glasgow merchant community is shown by the establishment in 1667 of a new harbour and town downriver at Port Glasgow.

Towards the end of the seventeenth century exports of wool declined but this was partly compensated by an expansion in the grain and cattle trades. Scottish cattle and sheep had been sold to

England before 1603 but the pacification of the Borders after the Union provided a boost to the trade. There was a steady increase in demand for meat from England's urban population and from the navy. Records for the Border customs precincts between 1680 and 1691 show that in some years around 30,000 cattle and rather more sheep were crossing to England. The manufacture of woollen plaiding did not recover to its early seventeenth century levels but the linen industry expanded substantially. Total exports to England by 1700 were probably between 1.2 and 1.8 million ells. Coal exports, after peaking in the 1660s, were lower and still falling in the 1690s but the production of salt was holding up and even expanding, although increasing competition in foreign markets and higher duties were restricting production to the domestic market.

Scotland continued to exhibit the classic weaknesses of an underdeveloped economy. Her limited range of exports rendered her vulnerable to shifts in overseas markets and competition from other producers. Members of Scotland's Parliament and Privy Council, well aware of the problems, passed a series of acts between the Restoration and the Union which represented a sustained attempt at economic improvement. Efforts to stimulate agriculture and industry, and to improve the balance of trade, were vigorous, if limited in their success. The continuity underlying this legislation, reaching back into the Covenanting period, is remarkable and suggests that there was a broad consensus, embracing magnates, lairds and merchants, regarding what needed to be done to improve the economy. The policy was a classic mercantilist one of conserving bullion by developing the domestic economy and trying to exclude imports that were a drain on foreign exchange while encouraging the export of manufactures where possible. The desire to imitate successful neighbours like England and Holland was understandable. The methods used to try and generate economic growth were, unfortunately, unrealistic.

Union and Expansion

The Revolution of 1688 marked the start of a period of increasing difficulty for the Scottish economy. War with France led to a loss of French markets and attacks by French privateers on Scottish shipping, even in coastal waters. A slump in textile production and rising taxation contributed to widespread impoverishment. Scottish merchants faced increasing difficulties as other European countries raised tariff barriers. The disastrous Darien Scheme caused a massive loss of capital among Scottish landowners and professional men. The long-term outlook for the economy seemed poor.

By the early years of the eighteenth century deteriorating Anglo-Scottish relations were threatening to disrupt the existing union. The part played by English opposition in wrecking the Darien venture highlighted the increasingly unworkable situation of two neighbouring kingdoms with competitive economic interests being ruled by the same monarch (Robertson, 1995). After 1689 the Scottish Parliament became increasingly assertive. In 1703 and 1704 it passed two acts in particular that alarmed English politicians. The Act of Security and Succession imposed major conditions on Scotland accepting the Hanoverian succession. The Act Anent Peace and War required the consent of the Scottish Parliament before war could be declared or treaties negotiated, allowing Scotland effectively to pursue an independent foreign policy. This legislation does not appear to have been designed to force an immediate split between the two countries but English politicians believed that this was the Scots' ultimate intention.

As late as 1702 English politicians' enthusiasm for a parliamentary union with Scotland was lukewarm at best. Now they revised their views. At first their aim was to ensure the Hanoverian succession within the framework of the Union of 1603. When it became clear that this would not be acceptable the case for closer union was considered. With the Scots taking such an independent line it did not seem likely that a loose federal system would be workable. The only feasible option was a full incorporating union. To achieve this it would be necessary to grant significant concessions to the Scots. The prospect of how the Scottish economy would fare in the event of a total breach with England helped to persuade many moderate Scots to look seriously at union with England. The Scots were also influenced by England's response to their legislation of 1703–4. In March

1705 the English Parliament passed an Alien Act, which stated that unless the Scots agreed by Christmas 1705 to start talks on negotiating an incorporating union, or had accepted the Hanoverian succession within the framework of the existing union, all Scots resident in England would be treated as aliens and their lands would be liable to seizure. The import of Scottish linen, coal and cattle into England would be banned and a blockade imposed to prevent Scottish trade with France.

This crude but effective blackmail was directed particularly at the Scottish nobility. A number of them had acquired English estates through marriage and many more were active in the cattle trade. Although the act was repealed in November 1705, the possibility that it could be reinstated remained. After initial fury in Scotland more careful consideration of the various options followed. There was general agreement about the depth of the economic crisis that Scotland was facing. The pro-unionists saw unhindered access to English markets, especially for cattle and linen, but also for grain, coal, salt and wool, as the only means of reversing economic decline. The view of the anti-unionists was that Scotland needed to improve her competitiveness in European markets in order to make herself independent of England.

There was little doubt that the economic understanding of the pro-unionists was sounder. It was all very well to suggest that Scotland should improve the quality of her exports but this had already been tried with limited success. Moreover, they made few constructive suggestions regarding how continental markets could be regained. In the more favourable climate of the 1670s it had been difficult enough to make such policies work. Thirty years later it was almost impossible.

The Union of 1707 remains one of the most controversial topics in Scottish history, one which continues to have relevance to modern political circumstances. Not only did it end Scotland's history as an independent state, but it has also been viewed as a major economic watershed. Much of Scotland's economic history during the seventeenth century has been seen, with hindsight, as leading inexorably towards union with England. For the eighteenth century the Union is often presented as an indispensible foundation for the economic and social progress that ultimately led to the Industrial Revolution. There has been considerable

debate concerning the motives that prompted Scots commissioners and parliamentarians to support or oppose union. One
view has emphasised Scotland's economic crisis as a major influence on the union debate. The other approach has focused on the
role of parties and political management in bringing about the
Union, relegating economic questions to the sidelines.

Ferguson (1977) has emphasised the importance of short-
term political manoeuvring in bringing about the Union,
suggesting that economic influences were only significant in
terms of how they were used to manipulate support. Space does
not permit discussion of the complex system of political management regulated by patronage, influence and self-interest by
which the Act of Union was brought about. But to ignore the fact
that the support of many influential Scots was bought by
pensions and payment of arrears of salary for various offices is to
ignore the reality of political life at this period.

The economic case has received renewed support in recent
years and has been persuasively argued by Whatley (1994,
'Bought and Sold'). There is no doubt about the importance of
English markets to Scottish trade. By the end of the seventeenth
century about half of Scottish exports went to England. This
emphasises the scale of the threat posed by the Alien Act but it
had already been foreshadowed by tariffs on coal and salt
imposed in 1698 and an increase on duries on Scottish linen. A
tightening up of restrictions from 1696 made illegal trade with
the American colonies much harder. Some interpretations have
suggested that rather than being close to collapse many of the
difficulties facing the Scottish economy were temporary rather
than a prelude to a major disaster that could have been avoided
only by Union. This may have been the case but it was not necessarily evident to contemporaries.

It has been appreciated that many Scots were reluctant to lose
control over their economic affairs and that from one point of
view Scotland's close trading links with England were the main
cause of its economic difficulties rather than a means of salvation.
As a counter to the political school of thought it has been
suggested that over-reliance on the private correspondence of key
political figures in the Union debate may be misleading. Operating over short timescales they may have taken the background

economic issues as given and focused instead on the minutiae of party politics.

The commissioners and many Scottish parliamentarians were landowners with a range of economic interests: cattle and corn, coal and salt, linen and woollens, herring and salmon. While the direct and indirect profits of political office were important landed wealth was still essential for most of them. Scottish politicians were closely in touch with economic conditions on their estates. All would benefit from continuing access to English markets; all would be threatened if this was to be withdrawn.

Economic matters played a direct and vital role in the Union debate. Fifteen of the 24 articles of Union were directly economic. Many of the concessions in the treaty favoured major landowners, in addition to direct bribes and indirect threats. The advantages of Union were manifest for the cattle trade and linen manufacture. In 1703 cattle accounted for 40 per cent of Scottish exports to England; linen was almost as important. There was also a need to safeguard the vulnerable sectors of the Scottish economy from English competition. The Scots were seeking protection as well as free trade. This was especially true of the coal and salt industries. It was once believed that these industries stood to gain from the Union through access to English markets. Whatley (1994, 'Nefs' Numbers') has shown, however, that they were increasingly tied to home markets in the late seventeenth century, and it was vital for Scotland that these markets should be retained. The 8th article of Union protected the Scottish salt industry from English competition. After 1707 salt making expanded, as did coal production.

It was the prospect of unrestricted trade with England rather than her colonies which was the main attraction of Union for most landowners and merchants. The burghs, rather than hoping for advantages from the Union, were scared by the threat of loss of trade if the treaty did not go through (Smout, 1987). The Darien disaster may have cooled enthusiasm for exotic foreign ventures and, given their limited resources, a successful trans-Atlantic trade would take time to build up. When capital was available it was already possible for Scottish vessels to trade with England's colonies. This was well appreciated by Glasgow's merchants who, despite their experience of trans-Atlantic trade, were solidly against union.

Some specific economic bribery was used to get the treaty through the Scottish Parliament. Six pro-Union members of parliament obtained private concessions exempting them from the general conditions of the treaty, including export duties on coal. Broader in scope was the promise of £2,000 sterling a year to encourage industry. A bigger bribe, aimed particularly at larger landowners, was the repayment of money lost in the Darien Scheme with 5 per cent interest. This was a tacit admission that England had helped to wreck the Darien Scheme and an acknowledgement of the economic harm this had done to Scotland. Taken together the measures amounted to a package of economic concessions designed to placate many who saw their interests threatened. The provisions were, overall, fair, and even generous in places. The safeguards incorporated into the treaty were almost all in favour of the Scots, something which was obviously aimed at securing its passage through the Scottish Parliament but which also emphasised that it was not an agreement between equals, that Scotland was the weaker partner.

What was the economic impact of the Union? Was it a major watershed? The traditional optimisic idea is that it brought political stability, strengthening the Revolution settlement of 1688–89. Closer links with England encouraged a flow of capital, technology and skills northwards. With the disappearance of the Scottish parliament the greater landowners turned increasingly towards economic development. Greater contact with more advanced and prosperous England provided a spur to modernisation and progress. There is an element of truth in these suggestions but they are too simplistic.

The Union was important to Scottish economic development but was not decisive on its own. The degree of continuity between the later seventeenth and eighteenth centuries is obscured by the crisis at the end of the century that helped to bring about the Union. The origins of agricultural change, more sophisticated business practices, along with government efforts to improve industry and the economy in general, as well as with the decay of the traditional framework of royal burgh privileges, all lie in the later seventeenth century. Commitment to improvement was already evident in embryonic form before 1707 in both the agricultural and industrial sectors. The basic causes of modernisation lay deep in Scottish society, reflecting an inheritance from before the Union. Factors such as education, religious attitudes and cultural values allowed the Scots to use the Union to their benefit. As was noted in Chapter 3 there was a steady convergence of Scottish culture with that of England in the later seventeenth century, which must have made the prospect of union more acceptable to many key figures. The Scots did not simply copy English ideas and technology; they made their own distinctive contribution to the Industrial Revolution, due in part to the more practical slant of Scottish education system.

There was a danger that Scotland might have become an economic dependency of England, a mere source of raw materials and cheap labour like Ireland, a fear that Andrew Fletcher of Saltoun expressed during the Union debate. One reason it did not was that English concern to bring about Union was based on political motives; there was little interest in the Scottish economy, whose backwardness prevented it from being seen as a threat to English industrial and commercial interests. While the backwardness of the Scottish economy provided protection against the more advanced economy of England, trying to keep Scotland stable and docile sometimes encouraged positive government measures such as the creation of the Board of Trustees for Manufactures in the wake of the malt tax riots of 1725.

In the short term the impact of Union was marginal. In the longer term it was a basic influence behind economic growth but only because Scottish society had, and continued, to develop the ability to exploit the opportunities that it offered. If the basic causes of modernisation of the Scottish economy after the 1740s were due to indigenous factors extending well back before 1707, the Union at least provided a context for them to develop successfully. In particular, the Union encouraged the Scottish economy towards developments that complemented rather than competed with England, as had been the case before 1707 in sectors like fine woollens.

The Union offered a new framework for Scottish economic development but no guarantees of success. Pro-Union pamphlets had generated unrealistic hopes for an immediate and dramatic spin-off from Union. These were, inevitably, dashed. The first two or three decades after 1707 demonstrated the disadvantages of Union, although they were not as dire as predicted. Taxation rose and the fine woollen industry was almost wiped out by English competition, although it had been in severe difficulties before 1707 anyway. Disillusion set in rapidly when the Union failed to generate an economic miracle. A new economic era remained only a propspect for some decades. Sir John Clerk of Penicuik, an enthusiastic pro-Unionist, recorded in 1730 his impressions of Scotland's progress since 1707. He had to admit that the Union seemed to have brought little benefit to Scotland. For 30 or 40 years after 1707 there is little evidence of significant economic growth. This is hardly surprising considering the essentially agrarian character of the Scottish economy overall. The stimulus of the English market was not significant until it, too, experienced substantial expansion, something that did not happen until the second half of the century. Economic expansion seems to have been nil before the 1720s and only began to improve markedly in the 1740s. Between was a period of modest growth.

Cattle and linen exports grew during the first half of the eighteenth century but livestock rearing fitted into the traditional economy and could be expanded without structural change. Numbers of cattle driven to England are recorded only sporadically and imperfectly but they seem to have risen from c.30,000 a year in the early eighteenth century to c.80,000 in the 1750s (Whyte, 1979; Lythe and Butt, 1975). It was only in the 1740s that the increased sale of linen production began to cause the industry to separate from its agricultural origins. The growth of the tobacco trade might seem to have been founded more securely on the Union. Tobacco imports to the Clyde grew only sluggishly in the years following 1707. This was not due to a lack of enterprise in Glasgow but to other factors, such as the stagnation of production in the colonies. However, official figures underestimate the real scale of imports due to the scale of smuggling. It is now believed that between 1715 and 1717, for example, smuggled imports were equivalent to as much as 62 per cent of legal imports due to underweighing of cargoes on a grand scale. Glasgow merchants were paying duty on only half to two thirds of the tobacco they imported and they also had interests in tobacco brought into London. As the scale of smuggling fell off in later decades the trade can now be seen to have grown earlier than previously thought and a little less fast in the middle decades of the century. The most recent history of Glasgow has emphasised that the scale of development of industry and trade between the later seventeenth century and *c*.1740 was greater than many previous historians have allowed (Devine and Jackson, 1995).

The Union did not, however, influence the tobacco trade directly. It had started before the Union and did not expand markedly until much later. Nevertheless, it is highly unlikely that without the Union England would have permitted Glasgow to develop the trade as it did. It has been suggested by some historians that, as an entrepôt trade, the tobacco trade was a mere enclave within the traditional economy, with little spin-off into other sectors. More recent research has demonstrated that the trade did have significant multiplier effects. The use of the direct purchase system by Scottish merchants required return cargoes for the plantations, leading to investment by Glasgow merchants in a range of industrial enterprises, especially textiles and coal mining. The trade also encouraged the development of banking and finance. The purchase of estates by prosperous merchants may have had some links with agricultural improvement. The effect of the tobacco merchants on agricultural improvement was, however, mostly indirect by encouraging economic expansion and the growth of urban population and a larger local market for agricultural produce. The need for capital to finance the trade led to widespread investment by middling groups: other merchants, professional men and smaller landowners. This spread the profits beyond the small merchant élite that dominated the trade. By the 1750s it was not just the middle classes who were benefitting; wages in west-central Scotland were significantly higher than in other areas.

Grain prices began to rise from *c*.1710. By the end of the 1760s they were over 50 per cent higher than they had been at the start of the century. This was not a spectacular improvement but may have been significant in terms of long-term capital accumulation by farmers and landowners. English grain prices fell from the 1660s to reach a low point between 1730 and 1750. In Scotland the late seventeenth-century fall was more marked but recovery came earlier. It has been suggested that there was no improvement in the productivity of Scottish agriculture between 1700 and the 1760s. Yet the structural changes highlighted by Devine, including the commutation of rents and the amalgamation of holdings, suggest that some improvement may have occurred. The slow but steady upward yield of crops on the mains of one Scottish estate, although hardly representative, suggests that higher yields could be obtained (Whyte, 1993). So several lines of evidence may suggest that economic performance was better in the years after 1707 than has sometimes been claimed. Population growth in eighteenth-century Scotland was moderate – slower than in England. This reduced the pressure on food supplies and allowed economic expansion. At the same time shortage of labour was avoided by structural change first in Lowland agriculture from the mid-eighteenth century and later by labour from the Highlands and Ireland (Devine, 1994).

Evidence of greater growth in the early decades of the eighteenth century is also evident in the coal industry (Whatley, 'Nef's numbers', 1994). Until recently, it has been suggested that the coal industry did not expand significantly in the first half of the eighteenth century. In the 1930s Professor Nef estimated total Scottish output in the later seventeenth century to be as high as 475,000 tons, a figure which has been generally accepted, with some reservations, by later historians. If Nef's figures are approximately correct, the Scottish coal industry must have expanded only modestly during the first 80 years of the eighteenth century and is unlikely to have provided much stimulus for growth in other sectors of the economy.

Recent work by Whatley (1994, 'Nef's numbers') has emphasised the shaky foundations on which Nef's estimates were based and has proposed a radical downwards revision of his figures. Whatley suggests that the amount of coal used in the salt industry was around 50,000 tons a year, perhaps as low as 40,000, rather than the 150,000 proposed by Nef, and that domestic consumption was also smaller. He calculates total output in the late seventeenth century at perhaps 225,000 tons a year, about half of Nef's figure, with production probably lower by 1700. On this basis the growth of the Scottish coal industry during the eighteenth century instead of being about ×4 was between ×8–×10, about twice the overall British rate, making Scotland one of the fastest-growing coal producing areas. In particular, there must have been much more rapid growth in output during the first half of the eighteenth century, as production by 1750 was at least 700,000 tons a year. Constraints on supply, such as technological difficulties, labour shortages, inefficient management and transport difficulties, have evidently been overstated. The Scottish coal industry can now be seen as having made a greater positive contribution to the early phases of Scottish industrialization, encouraging rather than checking growth.

The linen industry was the clearest success story in the first half of the eighteenth century. The quantity of linen stamped each year rose from 3.5 million yards in 1728 to 9 million by the mid-1750s. Exports to America grew from 92,715 yards in 1744 to 2,055,563 yards in 1760. Much of the output was of coarse cloth – ultimately it was cheap labour that made Scottish linen so competitive – but by the 1740s output of higher-quality linen was growing rapidly. As linen weaving became increasingly a full-time occupation rather than a part-time adjunct to agriculture the organisation of the industry became more complex. By the 1740s the size of firms was increasing steadily, with true factories beginning to appear.

That there was a considerable pool of underutilised talent and entrepreneurship in Scotland, the potential of which only started to be fully realised in the more encouraging post-Union climate, is suggested by the rise of the Clyde tobacco trade. It can also be demonstrated by the example of an individual career, that of Sir Archibald Grant of Monymusk (Cummings, 1994). In a later context J.M. Barrie said that there were few more impressive sights in the world than a Scotsman on the make. This was equally true of Grant. Aged 11 at the time of the Union, eldest son of a prominent legal and landowning family, he studied law and practised as an advocate in Edinburgh for several years. There, in a pre-Union context, he would probably have stayed. However, election to parliament in 1722 provided a wider stage for his abilities and ambitions. He was soon appointed a director of the notorious York Buildings Company, which had wide interests in the development of forfeited Jacobite estates (Chapter 5). Grant was also involved in mining ventures in Derbyshire, Wales and Norway, as well as in the West

Highlands. His involvement in the dubious world of corporate finance eventually enmeshed him in a major financial scandal that led to his expulsion from Parliament in 1732 and the end of his career in public life. He retired to Monymusk to make a name for himself as an agricultural improver. Despite his ultimate downfall Grant's career highlights the scale of opportunities that closer contact with England after 1707, along with access to English and colonial markets, offered ambitious Scots. The way south, which had been pioneered by the cronies of James VI, became, by the mid-eighteenth century, Samuel Johnson's famous high road.

By the 1760s Scots were starting to acquire power and influence within Great Britain to a degree which seemed disproportionate to some Englishmen. Scots had been going to England for centuries but never before in such numbers or with so much influence. By the 1760s the Scottish economy was starting to expand faster, in some respects, than that of England. Scottish universities were turning out far more trained professionals that Oxford and Cambridge; it was inevitable that many of them should go south in search of opportunity. The army provided an outlet for younger sons of Scottish landed families. By the mid-eighteenth century one army officer in four was Scots. The massive expansion of the empire after the Seven Years' War created many more openings in colonial administration, especially in India, which were eagerly seized by Scots. They infiltrated the highest levels of the British civil establishment more slowly but were starting to make significant inroads even here by the 1760s. The Scots may, in the main, have been reluctant partners to Union but within two generations it was providing a far wider stage for their talents and ambitions than an independent Scotland could ever have done (Colley, 1992).

CONCLUSION

By *c.*1760 the Scottish aristocracy had gone a long way towards assimilation with the English nobility, a process that had been under way gradually since the Reformation. In focusing their interests on a wider setting they had left Scotland increasingly under the immediate control of the gentry and the lesser nobility, together with the legal profession. Nevertheless, the system of patronage and political management still allowed them to run Scotland from London. The landed élite had progressively shed its feudal distinctions and was now forming an increasingly homogeneous group, in firm control of its lands and of the people inhabiting them. Many landowners were already making significant changes to the running of their estates and, imbued with the ethos of improvement, were on the verge of setting in motion changes that would transform the face of the countryside and drastically alter the structure of rural society within a couple of generations. That such changes were possible, with the co-operation rather than the opposition of the bulk of the tenantry, demonstrates the strength of control of twhe landowning élite over Scottish society and emphasises the degree to which society had changed from its violent sixteenth century image. A major influence behind this was the power of the church over many aspects of everyday life. But the church itself was changing as it sought to adapt to a more secularised society. The Highlands remained a region characterised by a different language and culture, but one which by 1760 was rapidly being transformed economically and socially as it was integrated into the British state. From being a problem region, the most significant source of Jacobite rebellions during the first half of the eighteenth century, the area's surplus manpower was, by the 1760s, being harnessed to provide troops to extend Britain's empire. By the 1760s too Scottish society had become markedly more urbanised with a greater proportion of her population dependent, either full or part time, on income from industrial activity. If the benefits of Union were a long time coming they were now clearly evident.

By the 1760s Scotland's society and economy were changing ever faster, at a pace that would have astonished observers from earlier centuries. Yet, as this book has attempted to show, while the pace of change may have accelerated markedly in the middle decades of the eighteenth century this transformation owed its origins to more gradual, less clearly defined and less well recorded changes that had occurred during the sixteenth and seventeenth centuries. These changes were complex and interconnected. The themes that have been developed here follow only some of the main strands. It is hoped, however, that in the space available something of the distinctive nature of early-modern Scotland's society and economy has been conveyed. Despite the surge of recent research many fundamental questions about Scottish society still remain to be posed, far less tackled and satisfactorily answered. If something of the excitment of the new work by social and economic historians in this field has been conveyed and some important potential directions for new research indicated, this book will have served a useful purpose.

FURTHER READING

General

The most recent one-volume general history of Scotland is M. Lynch *Scotland: a New History* (Edinburgh, 1991). The *New History of Scotland* covers the period in three volumes: J. Wormald *Court, Kirk and Community: Scotland 1470–1625* (London, 1981); R. Mitchison *Lordship to Patronage: Scotland 1603–1746* (London, 1983); B. Lenman *Integration, Enlightenment and Industrialization. Scotland 1746–1832* (London, 1989). More specifically concerned with social and economic issues, T.C. Smout *A History of the Scottish People 1560–1830* (London, 1969) is still in a class of its own. For a recent survey see I.D. Whyte *Scotland before the Industrial Revolution: an Economic and Social History c.1050–c.1750* (London, 1995). The debate 'Whither Scottish History'? in the *Scottish Historical Review,* **73** (1994), contains useful review articles and responses on early-modern and eighteenth-century Scotland. See also I. Donnachie and C. Whatley (eds) *The Manufacture of Scottish History* (Edinburgh, 1992).

Introduction

For comparative work on Scotland and Ireland see L.M. Cullen and T.C. Smout (eds) *Comparative Aspects of Irish and Scottish Economic and Social History* (Edinburgh, 1977), T.M. Devine and D. Dickson (eds) *Ireland and Scotland 1600–1850* (Edinburgh, 1983), R. Mitchison and P. Roebuck (eds) *Economy and Society in Scotland and Ireland 1500–1939* (Edinburgh, 1988) and S.J. Connolly, R.A. Houston and R.J. Morris (eds) *Conflict, Identity and Economic Development. Ireland and Scotland 1600–1939* (Preston, 1995). For comparisons with England see R.A. Houston and I.D. Whyte (eds) *Scottish Society 1500–1800* (Cambridge, 1989).

Chapter 1. Lord and Laird

R. Mitchison *Lordship to Patronage: Scotland 1603–1746* (London 1983). K.M. Brown *Kingdom or Province? Scotland and the Regal Union 1606–1715* (London, 1992) surveys some features of the Scottish nobility. A. Grant *Independence and Nationhood: Scotland 1306–1469*

(London, 1984) discusses the relative persistence of Scottish noble families. M. Meikle 'Lairds and Gentlemen: a Study of the Landed Families of the Eastern Anglo-Scottish Borders c1540–1603', unpublished PhD thesis, Edinburgh, 1988, provides a detailed view of interactions within landed society at a regional scale. See also M. Meikle 'The Invisible Divide: the Greater Lairds and the Nobility of Jacobean Scotland', *Scottish Historical Review*, **71** (1992), 70–87. Bonds of manrent are covered by J. Wormald *Lords and Men in Scotland: Bonds of Manrent 1442–1603* (Edinburgh, 1985). Relations between the nobility and the crown have been examined by M. Lee *John Maitland of Thirlestane and the Foundation of the Stewart Despotism in Scotland* (London, 1959), M. Lee *Government by Pen* (London, 1980), M. Lee *The Road to Revolution* (London, 1985), M. Lee 'Scotland and the "General Crisis" of the Seventeenth Century', *Scottish Historical Review*, **63** (1984), 136–54. For the rise of the lairds in Parliament during the later sixteenth century see J. Goodare 'Parliament and Society in Scotland 1560–1603', unpublished PhD thesis, Edinburgh, 1989. The financial state of the nobility is reviewed by K.M. Brown 'Noble Indebtedness in Scotland Between the Reformation and the Revolution', *Historical Research*, **62** (1989), 260–75, and K.M. Brown 'Aristocratic Finances and the Origins of the Scottish Revolution', *English History Review*, **104** (1989), 46–87. The anglicisation of the nobility is considered by K.M. Brown 'Courtiers and Cavaliers. Service, Anglicisation and Loyalty among the Royalist nobility', in J. Morrill (ed.) *The Scottish National Covenant in its British Context 1638–51* (Edinburgh, 1990), K.M. Brown 'The Scottish Aristocracy, Anglicisation and the Court 1603–38', *Historical Journal*, **36** (1993), 643–76, D. Stevenson 'The English Devil of Keeping State: Elite Manners and the Downfall of Charles I in Scotland', in R. Mason and N. Macdougall (eds) *People and Power in Scotland* (Edinburgh, 1992), 155–92. The deteriorating relationship between the nobility and Charles I is covered by A. Macinnes *Charles I and the Making of the Covenanting Movement* (Edinburgh, 1991) as well as by Lee (1985), *op. cit.* See also J. Goodare 'The Nobility of the Absolutist State in Scotland 1584–1638', *History*, **78** (1993), 161–82. The suggestion that revolution was the product of a general crisis in Scottish society is considered by E.J. Cowan 'The Making of the National Covenant', in J. Morrill (ed.) *The Scottish National Covenant in its British Context 1638–51* (Edinburgh, 1990), 69–89, and by W. Makey *The Church of the Covenant* (Edinburgh, 1979). The Scottish Revolution has been chronicled by D. Stevenson *The Scottish Revolution 1637–44* (Newton Abbot, 1973) and D. Stevenson *Revolution and Counter Revolution in Scotland* (Belfast, 1977). See also D. Stevenson 'The Financing of the Cause of the Covenants 1638–51', *Scottish Historical Review*, **51** (1972), 89–123, and 'The Effects of Revolution and Conquest on Scotland', in

R. Mitchison and P. Roebuck (eds) *Economy and Society in Scotland and Ireland 1500–1939* (Edinburgh, 1988), 48–57. R. Marshall *The Days of Duchess Anne* (London, 1973) looks at life in a late seventeenth-century noble household. The power structures of post-Union Scotland are dealt with by J. Shaw *The Management of Scottish Society 1704–1764* (Edinburgh, 1983) and A. Murdoch *The People Above* (Edinburgh, 1980).

Chapter 2. Landlord and Tenant

The sixteenth-century feuing movement is covered by M.H.B. Sanderson *Scottish Rural Society in the Sixteenth Century* (Edinburgh, 1982). For the patterns of landholding created by feuing and their eventual fate see R.A. Dodgshon *Land and Society in Early Scotland* (Oxford, 1981). W. Makey *The Church of the Covenant* (Edinburgh, 1979) suggests the possibility of a 'rural revolution' in sixteenth- and early seventeenth-century Scotland, although some of his ideas are challenged by A. Macinnes *Charles I and the Making of the Covenanting Movement* (Edinburgh, 1991). See also K.M. Brown's articles on noble finances cited for Chapter 1. The course of prices and wages is now securely established by A.J.S. Gibson and T.C. Smout *Prices, Food and Wages in Scotland 1550–1780* (Cambridge, 1995). Tenant mobility is discussed by I.D. Whyte and K.A. Whyte 'Continuity and Change in a Seventeenth-Century Scottish Farming Community', *Agricultural History Review*, **32** (1984), 159–69. Many aspects of seventeenth-century rural society are covered by I.D. Whyte *Agriculture and Society in Seventeenth-century Scotland* (Edinburgh, 1979). For changes in rural society from the late seventeenth century see T.M. Devine *The Transformation of Rural Scotland. Social Change and the Agrarian Economy 1660–1815* (Edinburgh, 1994). Holding size is also considered by R.A. Dodgshon (1981), *op. cit.* For farm reorganisation and depopulation in the Borders see R.A. Dodgshon 'Agricultural Change and its Social Consequences in the Southern Uplands of Scotland 1660–1780', in T.M. Devine and D. Dickson (eds) *Ireland and Scotland 1600–1850* (Edinburgh, 1983), 49–59. Capital accumulation by farmers in one community is considered by I.D. Whyte and K.A. Whyte 'Debt and Credit, Poverty and Prosperity in a Seventeenth-Century Scottish Rural Community', in R. Mitchison and P. Roebuck (eds) *Economy and Society in Scotland and Ireland 1500–1939* (Edinburgh, 1988), 70–80. Changing patterns of use of labour have been discussed by A. Gibson 'Proletarianism'? The Transition to Full-time Labour on a Scottish Estate 1723–1787, *Continuity and Change*, **5** (1990), 357–89. C. Whatley 'How tame were the Scottish Lowlanders during the Eighteenth century?', in T.M. Devine (ed.) *Conflict and Stability in Scottish Society 1700–1850* (Edinburgh, 1990), 1–30 discusses covert protest in rural society.

Chapter 3. Kirk and Culture

G. Marshall *Presbyteries and Profits* (Oxford, 1981) considers the possible relationships between Calvinism and economic development in Scotland. W. Makey *The Church of the Covenant* (Edinburgh, 1979) examines the wealth and social position of Scottish ministers. The operation and effects of kirk sessions are described by G. Parker 'The "Kirk by Law Established" and the Origins of "The Taming of Scotland": St Andrews 1559–1600', in L. Leneman (ed.) *Perspectives in Scottish Social History* (Aberdeen, 1988), 1–32, L.M. Smith 'Sackcloth for the Sinner or Punishment for the Crime? Church and Secular Courts in Cromwellian Scotland', in J. Dwyer, R.A. Mason and A. Murdoch (eds) *New Perspectives on the Politics and Culture of Early Modern Scotland* (Edinburgh, 1985) and R. Mitchison and L. Leneman *Sexuality and Social Control. Scotland 1660–1780* (Oxford, 1989). For poor relief see R. Mitchison 'The Making of the Old Scottish Poor Law', *Past and Present*, **63** (1974), 58–93. The survival of fire rituals is discussed by R.A. Dodgshon 'The Scottish Farming Township as a Metaphor', in L. Leneman (ed.) *Perspectives in Scottish Social History* (Aberdeen, 1988), 69–82. For civic ceremony see M. Lynch (ed.) *The Early Modern Scottish Town* (London, 1987). Church attendance is assessed by C. Brown *The Social History of Religion in Scotland Since 1730* (London, 1987) and R.A. Houston *Social Change in the Age of Enlightenment: Edinburgh 1660–1760* (Oxford, 1994). For education and literacy the definitive study is R.A. Houston *Scottish Literacy and the Scottish Identity* (London, 1985). For changes in the Scottish universities and élite culture in the later seventeenth century see H. Ouston 'York in Edinburgh: James VII and the Patronage of Learning in Scotland, 1679–1688', in J. Dwyer, R.A. Mason and A. Murdoch (eds) *New Perspectives on the Politics and Culture of Early Modern Scotland* (Edinburgh, 1985), 113–55, and R.L. Emerson 'Scottish Cultural Change 1660–1710 and the Union of 1707', in J. Robertson (ed.) *A Union for Empire* (Cambridge, 1995), 121–44. Changes in the church during the first half of the eighteenth century are discussed in C. Brown (1987), *op. cit.* and C. Brown *The People in the Pews* (Dundee, 1993). For religious revivalism see T.C. Smout 'Born again at Cambuslang', *Past and Present*, **97** (1982), 114–27. The rise of the Moderates is discussed by R.B. Sher *Church and University in the Scottish Enlightenment 1730–90* (Princeton, 1986). The literature on the Enlightenment is vast. The critical bibliography in Sher (1986) is a good starting point. See also J. Rendall *The Origins of the Scottish Enlightenment* (London, 1978), A. Chitnis *The Scottish Enlightenment: a Social History* (London, 1976), and R.H. Campbell and A. Skinner *The Origins and Nature of the Scottish Enlightenment* (Edinburgh, 1982). The social background to Enlightenment Edinburgh is explored by R.A. Houston (1994), *op.cit.*

Chapter 4. Centre and Locality

M. Meikle 'Lairds and Gentlemen: a Study of the Landed Families of the Eastern Anglo-Scottish Borders c1540–1603', unpublished PhD thesis, Edinburgh, 1988, provides a rare study of interactions within a specific locality. J. Goodare 'Parliament and Society in Scotland 1560–1603', unpublished PhD thesis, Edinburgh, 1989, is excellent on many aspects of centre–locality relationships in the later sixteenth century. For the workings of the Scottish judicial system at a local level see S.J. Davies 'The Courts and the Scottish Legal System 1600–1747: the Case of Stirlingshire', in V.A.C. Gatrell, B. Lenman and G. Parker (eds) *Crime and the Law* (London, 1980), 54–79. For relations between the crown and the nobility in the sixteenth century see J. Wormald *Court, Kirk and Community. Scotland 1470–1625* (London, 1981). Feuding has been covered by J. Wormald 'Bloodfeud, Kindred and Government in Early-Modern Scotland', *Past and Present,* **87** (1980), 54–97, J. Wormald *Lords and Men in Scotland. Bonds of Manrent 1442–1603* (Edinburgh, 1985) and K.M. Brown *Bloodfeud in Scotland 1573–1625* (Edinburgh, 1986). For comments on the lack of peasant revolts in Scotland see A. Grant *Independence and Nationhood. Scotland 1304–1469* (London, 1984). The sad case of Jean Livingstone is analysed by K.M. Brown 'The Laird, his Daughter, her Husband and the Minister: Unravelling a Popular Ballad', in R. Mason and N. MacDougall (eds) *People and Power in Scotland* (Edinburgh, 1992), 104–25. The pacification of the Border is covered by T.I. Rae *The Administration of the Scottish Frontier 1513–1603* (Edinburgh, 1966) and C.M.F. Ferguson 'Law and Order on the Anglo-Scottish Border 1603–1707', unpublished PhD thesis, St Andrews, 1981. For a readable but over-sensationalised view of Border raiding see G.M. Fraser *The Steel Bonnets* (London, 1971). The expansion of central government in late sixteenth-century Scotland is discussed by M. Lee *John Maitland of Thirlestane and the Foundation of the Stewart Despotism in Scotland* (London, 1959) and *Government by Pen* (London, 1980). For taxation see J. Goodare 'Parliamentary Taxation in Scotland 1560–1603', *Scottish Historical Review,* **68** (1989), 23–52. For the organisation of the Covenanters see A. Macinnes 'Scottish Gaeldom, 1638–1651: the Vernacular Response to the Covenanting Dynamic', in J. Dwyer, R.A. Mason and A. Murdoch (eds) *New Perspectives on the Politics and Culture of Early Modern Scotland* (Edinburgh, 1985), 59–94, and E. Furgol 'Scotland Turned Sweden: the Scottish Covenanters and the Military Revolution 1638–51', in J. Morrill (ed.) *The Scottish National Covenant in its British Context 1638–51* (Edinburgh, 1990), 134–54, as well as A. Macinnes 'The Scottish Constitution, 1638–51: the Rise of Oligarchic Centralism, in J. Morrill (1990), *op. cit.,* 106–33, and W. Makey *The Church of the Covenant* (Edinburgh, 1979). Aspects of crime and violence in the later seventeenth century are discussed by L. Leneman *Living in Atholl 1685–1785* (Edinburgh, 1986). For a more general view see C.A. Whatley 'An Uninflammable People?', in I. Donnachie and C. Whatley (eds) *The Manufacture of Scottish History* (Edinburgh, 1992), 51–71. For the eighteenth century see C.A. Whatley 'How Tame Were the Scottish Lowlanders During the Eighteenth Century?', in T.M. Devine (ed.) *Conflict and Stability in Scottish Society 1700–1850* (Edinburgh, 1990), 1–30. The occurrence and social significance of urban protest is analysed by R.A. Houston *Social Change in the Age of Enlightenment: Edinburgh 1660–1760* (Oxford, 1994). T.M. Devine, *The Transformation of Rural Scotland. Social Change and the Agrarian Economy 1660–1815* (Edinburgh, 1994), considers tenants' opposition to improvement.

Chapter 5. Highland and Lowland

The most recent study of the rise and fall of an individual clan is M.D.W. MacGregor 'A Political History of the MacGregors Before 1571', unpublished PhD thesis, Edinburgh, 1989. T.C. Smout *A History of the Scottish People 1560–1830* (London, 1969) provides a good general survey of clanship. For a challenging recent reinterpretation see R.A. Dodgshon 'Pretense of Blude and Plaice of thair Dwelling', in R.A. Houston and I.D. Whyte (eds) *Scottish Society 1500–1800* (Cambridge, 1989), 169–98. The integration of Highland and Island, as well as Highland and Lowland, is discussed by J.E.A. Dawson 'The Origins of the "Road to the Isles": Trade Communication and Campbell Power in Early Modern Scotland', in R. Mason and N. Macdougall (eds) *People and Power in Scotland* (Edinburgh, 1992), 74–103. The changing boundaries of the Gaidhealtachd are delimited by C.W.J. Withers *Gaelic in Scotland 1698–1981. The Geographical History of a Language* (Edinburgh, 1984). For changes in Highland society during the seventeenth century see D. Stevenson *Alastair MacColla and the Highland Problem in the Seventeenth Century* (Edinburgh, 1980), E.J. Cowan 'Clanship, Kinship and the Campbell Acquisition of Islay', *Scottish Historical Review*, **58** (1979), 132–57, and A.I. Macinnes 'Scottish Gaeldom 1638–1651: the Vernacular Response to the Covenanting Dynamic', in J. Dwyer, R.A. Mason and A. Murdoch (eds) *New Perspectives on the Politics and Culture of Early Modern Scotland* (Edinburgh, 1985), 59–94. Changing illegitimacy levels in the Highlands are discussed in R. Mitchison and L. Leneman *Sexuality and Social Control in Scotland 1660–1780* (Oxford, 1989). For changes in the Highland economy see R.A. Dodgshon *Land and Society in Early Scotland* (Oxford, 1981), 'Strategies of Farming in the Western Highlands and Islands of Scotland Prior to Crofting and the Clearances', *Economic History Review*,

46 (1993), 679–701, and 'The Ecological Basis of Highland Peasant Farming 1500–1800', in H.H. Birks, H.J.B.Birks, P.E. Kaland and D. Moe (eds) *The Cultural Landscape, Past, Present and Future* (Cambridge, 1988). The case study of the first Earl of Cromartie comes from E. Richards and M. Clough *Cromartie: Highland Life 1650–1914* (Aberdeen, 1989). For changes on the Argyll estates see E. Cregeen 'The Tacksmen and their Successors: a Study of Tenurial Reorganisation in Mull, Morvern and Tiree in the Early Eighteenth Century', *Scottish Studies*, **13** (1969), 93–145, and I.G. Lindsay and M. Cosh *Inveraray and the Dukes of Argyll* (Edinburgh, 1972). Industrial activity in the Highlands in the early eighteenth century is reviewed by A.J.G. Cummings 'Industry and Investment in the Eighteenth Century Highlands: The York Buildings Company of London', in A.J.G. Cummings and T.M. Devine (eds) *Industry, Business and Society in Scotland Since 1700* (Edinburgh, 1994), 24–42. For the work of the Forfeited Estates commissioners see A. Smith *Jacobite Estates of the Forty Five* (Edinburgh, 1982). Gaelic culture in Lowland Scottish towns is discussed by C.W.J. Withers 'Kirk, Club and Culture Change. Gaelic Chapels, Highland Societies and the Urban Gaelic Subculture in Eighteenth Century Scotland', *Social History*, **10** (1985), 171–92. For a recent survey of long-term change in the Highlands see A.I. Macinnes 'Landownership, Land Use and Elite Enterprise in Scottish Gaeldom: from Clanship to Clearance in Argyllshire 1688–1858', in T.M. Devine (ed.) *Scottish Elites* (Edinburgh, 1994), 1–42. For more general studies of changes in the Highlands during the eighteenth century see C.W.J. Withers *Gaelic Scotland. The Transformation of a Culture Region* (London, 1988) and A.J. Youngson *After the Forty Five* (Edinburgh, 1973).

Chapter 6. Town and Country

Patterns of urbanisation in Scotland are discussed by I.D. Whyte 'Urbanisation in Early-Modern Scotland: a Preliminary Analysis', *Scottish Economic and Social History*, **9** (1989), 21–37, and M. Lynch 'Urbanisation and Urban Networks in Seventeenth Century Scotland', *Scottish Economic and Social History*, **12** (1991), 24–41. To set Scotland in a European perspective see J. de Vries *European Urbanization 1500–1800* (London, 1985). The best overall survey of early-modern Scottish urban development are the essays in M. Lynch (ed.) *The Early-Modern Town in Scotland* (London, 1987). For the development of Old Aberdeen as a baronial burgh see R. Tyson 'The Economic and Social Structure of Old Aberdeen in the Seventeenth Century', in J.S. Smith (ed.) *Old Aberdeen* (Aberdeen, 1991), 38–56. The impact of the Revolution on Scottish towns is discussed by D. Stevenson 'The Burghs and the Scottish Revolution', in M. Lynch (1987), *op. cit.*, 167–91. The agricultural side of a regional centre like Dumfries is considered by W. Coutts 'Provincial Merchants and Society: a Study of Dumfries Based on the Registers of Testaments 1600–1665', in M. Lynch (1987), *op.cit.*, 147–66, as well as I.D. Whyte *Agriculture and Society in Seventeenth Century Scotland* (Edinburgh, 1979) and I.D. Whyte 'The Occupational Structure of Scottish Burghs in the late Seventeenth Century', in M. Lynch (1987), *op. cit.*, 219–44. The case study of the Dundas estates is in I.D. Whyte 'Infield–Outfield Farming on a Seventeenth Century Scottish Estate', *Journal of Historical Geography*, 5 (1979), 391–402. Farm structures in Edinburgh's hinterland are described in T.M. Devine *The Transformation of Rural Scotland* (Edinburgh, 1994) and the shift from grain to livestock in R.A. Dodgshon *Land and Society in Early Scotland* (Oxford, 1981). For the provision of credit see H. Booton 'John and Andrew Cadiou: Aberdeen Notaries of the Fifteenth and Early Sixteenth Centuries', *Northern Scotland*, 9 (1982), 17–20, and D. Macniven 'Merchant and Trader in Early Seventeenth Century Aberdeen', unpublished MLitt thesis, Aberdeen, 1977. The activities of the Edinburgh merchant élite in the early seventeenth century have been analysed by J.J. Brown 'The Social, Political and Economic Influence of the Edinburgh Merchant Elite 1600–38', unpublished PhD thesis, Edinburgh, 1985. For the grain trade see I.D. Whyte *Agriculture and Society* (1979), *op. cit.*, and for new market centres I.D. Whyte 'The Growth of Periodic Market Centres in Scotland 1600–1707', *Scottish Geographical Magazine*, 95 (1979), 13–26. The case study of Alloa has been discussed by T.C. Smout 'The Erskines of Mar and the Development of Alloa 1689–1825', *Scottish Studies*, 7 (1963), 57–74. For population mobility see R.A. Houston 'Geographical Mobility in Scotland 1652–1811', *Journal of Historical Geography*, 11 (1985), 379–94. For the effect of the 1690s famines on Aberdeen see R.E. Tyson 'Famine in Aberdeenshire 1695–9: Anatomy of a Crisis', in D. Stevenson (ed.) *From Lairds to Louns* (Aberdeen, 1986), 32–52. The impact of the Cromwellian garrison is discussed by G. Desbrisay 'Menacing their Persons and Exacting on their Purses: The Aberdeen Justice Court 1657–1700', in D. Stevenson (1986), *op. cit.*, 70–90. Patterns of apprenticeship migration to Edinburgh are analysed by A. Lovett, I.D. Whyte and K.A. Whyte 'Poisson Regression Analysis and Migration Fields. The Example of the Apprenticeship Records of Edinburgh in the Seventeenth and Eighteenth Centuries', *Transactions of the Institute of British Geographers*, NS, 10 (1985), 317–32. Patterns of female migration to Edinburgh are examined in I.D. Whyte and K.A. Whyte 'The Geographical Mobility of Women in Early-Modern Scotland', in L. Leneman (ed.) *Perspectives in Scottish Social History* (Aberdeen, 1988), 83–106. For marriage patterns in East Lothian see I.D. Whyte 'Marriage and Mobility in East Lothian in the Seventeenth and Eighteenth Centuries', *Transactions of the East Lothian Antiquarian Society*, 19 (1987),

17–30. Highland migration to lowland towns is considered by C.W.J. Withers 'Highland Migration to Dundee, Perth and Stirling 1753–1891', *Journal of Historical Geography*, **11** (1985), 395–418. For the industrial specializations of the main Scottish towns see M. Lynch (1987), *op. cit.* Aberdeen is also considered by D. Macniven (1977), *op. cit.*, and R.E. Tyson 'The Rise and Fall of Manufacturing in Rural Aberdeenshire', in J.S. Smith and D. Stevenson (eds) *Fermfolk and Fisherfolk* (Aberdeen, 1989), 63–82. The case study of Elgin is J.E. Thomas 'Elgin Notaries in Burgh Society and Government 1540–1660', *Northern Scotland*, **13** (1993), 21–30. A recent major study of the social and occupational structure of Edinburgh is H. Dingwall *Late Seventeenth Century Edinburgh: a Demographic Study* (Aldershot, 1994). The role of education in the capital is discussed in R.A. Houston 'Literature, Education and the Culture of Print in Enlightenment Edinburgh', *History*, **78** (1993), 373–92. Less detail is available for Glasgow but see T.M. Devine and G. Jackson (eds) *Glasgow Vol. 1. Beginnings to 1830* (Manchester, 1995). For Aberdeen in the early sixteenth century see H. Booton 'The Craftsmen of Aberdeen Between 1400 and 1550', *Northern Scotland*, **13** (1993), 1–19.

Chapter 7. Economic Decline and Growth

For general background see S.G.E. Lythe *The Economy of Scotland in its European Setting 1550–1625* (Edinburgh, 1963) and T.C. Smout *Scottish Trade on the Eve of Union, 1660–1707* (Edinburgh, 1963), S.G.E. Lythe and J. Butt *An Economic History of Scotland 1100–1939* (Glasgow, 1975). See also T.M. Devine and S.G.E. Lythe 'The Economy of Scotland under James VI', *Scottish Historical Review*, **50** (1971), 91–106. Patterns of late-medieval trade are discussed by I. Guy 'The Scottish Export Trade 1460–1599', in T.C. Smout (ed.) *Scotland and Europe 1200–1850* (Edinburgh, 1986), 62–81. The proposals for Union after 1603 are discussed in B. Galloway *The Union of England and Scotland 1603–8* (Edinburgh, 1986) For Government intervention in the economy in the late sixteenth century see T. Goodare 'Parliament and Society in Scotland 1560–1603', unpublished PhD thesis, Edinburgh, 1989. For urban–rural contrasts see R.A. Dodgshon *Land and Society in Early Scotland* (Oxford, 1981). For Charles I's fishery scheme see A. Macinnes *Charles I and the Making of the Covenanting Movement* (Edinburgh, 1991). The rise of Edinburgh's trade in the sixteenth century is discussed in M. Lynch (ed.) *The Early-Modern Scottish Town* (London, 1987). For the capital's merchant élite in the early seventeenth century see J.J. Brown 'The Social, Political and Economic Influences of the Edinburgh Merchant elite 1600–38', unpublished PhD thesis, Edinburgh, 1985. For the effects of the Revolution on the Scottish economy see D. Stevenson 'The

Effects of Revolution and Conquest on Scotland', in R. Mitchison and P. Roebuck (eds) *Economy and Society in Scotland and Ireland 1500–1939* (Edinburgh, 1988), 48–58, and T.M. Devine 'The Cromwellian Union and the Scottish Burghs: the Case of Aberdeen and Glasgow 1652–60', in J. Butt and J.T.Ward (eds) *Scottish Themes* (Edinburgh, 1976), 1–16. For a reassessment of Glasgow mercantile activity in the late seventeenth century see T.M. Devine and G. Jackson (eds) *Glasgow Vol.1 Beginnings to 1830* (Manchester, 1995). For late seventeenth-century agricultural improvement see I.D. Whyte *Agriculture and Society in Seventeenth-Century Scotland* (Edinburgh, 1979). The Union continues to generate debate. For a recent set of essays see J. Robertson (ed.) *A Union for Empire* (Cambridge, 1995). The political interpretation of the Union is put forcefully in W. Ferguson *Scotland's Relations with England: a Survey to 1707* (Edinburgh, 1977) and P.W.J. Riley *The Union of Scotland and England* (Manchester, 1978). For the economic case see Smout (1963), *op. cit.*, and C.A. Whatley 'Bought and Sold for English Gold?' (Edinburgh, 1994). The burghs' view of the Union is discussed by T.C. Smout 'The Burgh of Montrose and the Union of 1707: a Document', *Scottish Historical Review,* **66** (1987), 183–4. For post-Union economic growth see T.M. Devine and G.Jackson (1995), *op. cit.*; T.M. Devine 'The Union of 1707 and Scottish Development, *Scottish Economic and Social History,* **5** (1985), 23–40; C.A. Whatley 'New Light on Nef's Numbers: Coal Mining and the First Phase of Scottish Industrialisation c1700–1830', in A.J.G. Cummings and T.M. Devine (eds) *Industry, Business and Society in Scotland Since 1700* (Edinburgh, 1994), 2–23; T.M. Devine *The Tobacco Lords* (Edinburgh, 1975); and A.J. Durie *The Scottish Linen Industry in the Eighteenth Century* (Edinburgh, 1979). For increases in crop yields see I.D. Whyte 'Crop Yields on the Mains of Yester. 1698–1753', Transactions of the East Lothian Antiquarian Society, **22** (1993), 23–30. On a broader scale see R.H. Campbell *Scotland Since 1707: the Rise of an Industrial Society* (Edinburgh, 1985) and T.C. Smout 'Where had the Scottish Economy got to by the Third Quarter of the Eighteenth century?', in I. Hont and M. Ignatieff (eds) *Wealth and Virtue* (Cambridge, 1983), 45–72. The case study of Sir Archibald Grant is by A.J.G. Cummings 'The Business Affairs of an Eighteenth Century Lowland Laird: Sir Archibald Grant of Monymusk 1696–1778', in T.M. Devine (ed.) *Scottish Elites* (Edinburgh, 1994), 43–61. For the infiltration of Scots into England and the empire see L. Colley *Britons: Forging the Nation 1707–1837* (London, 1992).

INDEX

Index